NOTICE

of

RELEASE

A Daughter's Journey to
Forgive her Mother's Killer

STEPHANIE CASSATLY

a memoir

eLectio Publishing

Little Elm, TX

www.eLectioPublishing.com

Notice of Release: A Daughter's Journey to Forgive Her Mother's Killer
By Stephanie Cassatly

Copyright 2017 by Stephanie Cassatly. All rights reserved.
Cover Design by eLectio Publishing.

ISBN-13: 978-1-63213-288-8

Published by eLectio Publishing, LLC
Little Elm, Texas
http://www.eLectioPublishing.com

Printed in the United States of America

5 4 3 2 1 eLP 21 20 19 18 17

The eLectio Publishing creative team is comprised of: Kaitlyn Campbell, Emily Certain, Lori Draft, Court Dudek, Jim Eccles, Sheldon James, and Christine LePorte.

Publisher's Note

The publisher does not have any control over and does not assume any responsibility for author or third-party websites or their content.

Praise for Stephanie Cassatly's *Notice of Release*

Stephanie Cassatly's redemptive memoir is a great gift to humanity. Chronicling her mother's life and death and the progression of her own forgiving heart, the book moves from capsizing grief to a place of hope, healing and strength. This compelling transformative narrative is important reading for anyone seeking to make meaning out of trauma, deal with unresolved pain or simply better understand the healing power of forgiveness.

—Marina Catacuzino
Founder of *The Forgiveness Project*
Author of *Stories for a Vengeful Age*

Notice of Release explores the boundaries of grief—and, just as importantly, forgiveness—ultimately finding common ground between the two. Cassatly untangles the threads of the actions of the man who killed her mother, revealing connections to family dynamics, culture, class, and identity. Any good book about death is a *memento mori*, reminding the reader about the nature of mortality. *Notice of Release* combines the certainty of death with the uncertainty of forgiveness. Cassatly travels a great emotional distance to find empathy, and her journey is all the more powerful for that. This is a beautiful, very human book.

—Sue William Silverman
Author, *The Pat Boone Fan Club:*
My Life as a White Anglo-Saxon Jew

Who can ever be prepared for a no-cause/no-reason murder of a mother (or anyone, for that matter)? The thought makes reason stare. But Stephanie Cassatly takes her reader, step-by-step, through the painful process of forgiveness. In doing so, she opens the door for those wanting to enlarge their understanding and, maybe, their heart.

Phyllis Barber
Author, *To The Mountain*

For Michael, Hannah and Sarah

CONTENTS

God's grace is a breeze that blows continuously.
We simply have to set our sail to catch it.

~ Swami Prabhavanda

Prologue
(2015)

Twenty-four years after my mother was killed, I went to Louisiana State Penitentiary, better known as Angola, to visit the place her killer served his life sentence and died. It was a bleak and cloudy day when I arrived at the imposing gates of the maximum-security prison, 900 miles from my home in Florida. As a writer and a victim, I'd arranged a tour of the prison, including his grave in "Point Look Out Cemetery," a tranquil plot of land on the rural prison farm at the foot of the Tunica hills. The serene name of this burial ground implied a final place from where to reflect upon one's life. And there was much to reflect upon in both his life and mine. Although I'd come feeling uncertain of my emotions, there was an unexpected peace that washed over me at the end of the tour, as I walked through the arched trellis entrance conjoining a white picket fence surrounding rows of hundreds of small white concrete crosses. I thought that by coming here I had orchestrated the perfect ending to my story.

My mother's death changed every predetermined notion I had about the world and what it meant to feel safe. It informed everything thereafter, including intimate relationships, motherhood, career, and friendships. Before she died, I'd always thought that murder was something that happened in the news, in far away places, to other people, and that I was somehow immune to such ugly things. I was mistaken.

To this day, I cannot visit New Orleans without feeling the weight of losing my mother. She is in the scent of every flowering magnolia, the moist air that drapes the city, the soulful jazz of the French Quarter, the rich taste of red beans and rice and the steady current of the Mississippi River. She is everywhere, yet nowhere, an illusive shadow.

Like living on two different continents, my life before and my life after her death bore no resemblance to each other, and it has taken me most of my life to adjust to living in the second. In my forties, I

1

realized that in order to continue the life I was trying to create with my husband and two daughters, I had to go back and unearth my mother and father's stories, as well as the story of my mother's killer, in order to understand what had happened and why. Years of avoiding the topic of her death, even her killer's name, had not abated my nightmares and anxiety. Although satisfied that justice had been served, I wondered how much had been gained. Still in so much pain, there was no way to fill the crater that her death had left in my life and nowhere to turn for peace. Just before her killer died in prison in 2000, in an act almost as difficult and mysterious as her death, I reached out and forgave him. It was then that I realized that I had been as much of a prisoner as he was.

Although I did not understand anything about the universal and transformative nature of forgiveness until many years later, long after her killer died and when I began writing my story, the words of a global peacemaker, Archbishop Desmond Tutu, have clarified much for me. A friend gave me a small book of his, *The Book of Forgiving*. In it, he shares the African concept of Ubuntu, "I am me, because you are you," stressing our interconnected humanity, the truths on both sides of a story and how after violence and pain, only forgiveness enables people to fully move forward. He also says, "there is no future without forgiveness," which only now do I realize was true for me.

Forgiving my mother's killer, however, was a complex process, not a quick or tidy proposition. To mistake it for anything less would be akin to giving up an organ or a limb and then regretting it. Offering forgiveness prematurely, or with the wrong understanding, risks deepening a wound and victimizing one further. The process had a life of its own, which I could not control or rush. There were many steps along my journey, and I have tried to give them form in the following words.

Writing this book has been my road map, my true north, and my grace. Through many complicated emotions, worrying about my privacy and that of my family, researching, digging and sometimes obsessing, I realize I am not alone on this journey. Many others carry the weight of violent losses and seemingly deep and irreconcilable hurts. Although it has taken me many years, through many twists and turns, I want to let others know that there is a way out of the darkness. Forgiveness was my way.

One
Angola
(2004)

Rural Highway 66 stretches endlessly toward the horizon, a blurry wave rising above the hot tar as far as I can see. Dried wheat grass, burnt by the unforgiving sun, lines the edge of this two-lane road running through the Louisiana lowlands. Small towns dot the way: Baton Rouge, Port Hudson, St. Francisville, Tunica. Busy towns give way to rolling pastures of willows and magnolias with cows grazing beneath them. Pecan orchards contour the hills in slightly crooked rows leading up to historic plantation homes. These estates whisper century-old stories of privilege and slavery, love and hatred, of war and peace.

It's a two-hour drive from New Orleans to Angola. I have an appointment to meet the ghost of Nathan Wolfe, the man who murdered my mother twenty-four years ago. As I drive west, I will myself to focus on the road ahead and not behind, but this road contains my history, where dreams and reflections haunt me, calling my name, luring me beyond comprehension or reason. Reckless, but steadfast. I listen. I follow. I'm under their command.

Running low on gas, I turn into a dilapidated roadside station. When the engine stops, I open the door to the shrill sound of cicadas filling the humid summer air. The attendant, an old, dark-skinned man, tall and with a limp, walks toward me. I can't tell which leg is damaged.

"How much farther to Angola?" I ask, standing to stretch my legs.

He rubs his cheek, slow in thought. His skin is cracked like a dry riverbed. "Oh, dawlin' you still got a ways to go. Maybe another hour," he says. "Where you come from?"

"New Orleans. This morning," I say, unwilling to offer up much more.

5

"Not too far, I guess. A city girl comin' out to da country, eh?" He laughs. I nod.

He feels familiar to me, his uniform of navy blue pants and light blue shirt with his name imprinted on the pocket, the smell of his corncob pipe filled with cherry tobacco. He feels like my childhood summers spent along the edge of the Mississippi River at my grandparents' home. My grandfather, Papa Luke, who wore the same uniform and smelled of cherry tobacco, had lighter skin and worked as a janitor at a local school. Papa Luke, an immigrant from Italy, had poor command of English. My mother once confided that he couldn't read or write, which only endeared him to me more.

I hand the attendant the money, thank him for his help and get back into my car. Gradually, the terrain stretches out into flatland. I settle comfortably into my seat, and relish the ease of a straighter road.

Over the years, I have revisited my mother's story again and again. If it were just her story, perhaps I could settle on an ending and simply leave it alone. But it's also my story, as much a part of my identity as the color of my eyes or hair. Whenever someone says, "Tell me about yourself," I'm always tempted to say that I'm in my early forties, married with two daughters, and my mother was murdered when I was eighteen. But of course I omit the last part with respect to social etiquette. Murder is a grisly subject. It makes people uncomfortable. So it remains the silent part of my identity, except to those who know me well. Still, I haven't been able to let go of it, no matter how hard I try. I always come back to it. Or it comes back to me. It's impossible to keep this sort of history at a distance. We are as twined as the strands of a rope. Maybe I keep revisiting the story not in search of an ending, but a different interpretation. Each time I return to it, the story feels slightly changed, and I am a different interpreter.

I've never set foot in a prison before. Not an operational one, anyway. Once, when I was a child, my family visited San Francisco where we toured historic Alcatraz. On the ferryboat ride to the island, the prison loomed like a medieval castle. I imagined criminals trying to escape across the cold rough waters of San Francisco Bay. Other prisons I remembered seeing from the car window on family road trips. Large concrete complexes with spiral barbed-wire fences and armed guards in towers. They were mysterious and frightening to me, places I feared I'd end up if I ever stole anything or told a lie.

In retrospect, I think it strange I never before asked about Nathan Wolfe. It took twenty years for me to even learn his name. The solid expanse of my mother's absence had left no room for her killer's identity. His namelessness gave him great power over me, elevating him to a mythical monster, almost a god. Or perhaps I had simply befriended denial as my trusted guardian. Finally, two decades later, when I did ask, I wasn't sure I wanted to know about him, for fear of what might be unleashed.

My visit to Angola has been inspired by Father La Beauve, a soft-spoken Catholic priest with a Cajun accent, employed by the prison chaplain's office. He answered a phone call I placed several years ago from my home in Florida -- the first of several calls.

After our last conversation, I decided to visit Angola and conveniently dovetail the trip with a long overdue visit to family. My mother's three remaining sisters live only two hours away. It has been years since I've seen them. Career, children, family, fear – there was always something that kept me from returning to Louisiana, the place of my mother's birth, and also her untimely death.

Now, as I draw closer to Angola, the radio plays "Amazing Grace," by Elvis. I know this has significance, like the back music for a movie, the movie of my life. I wonder if I am envisioning the last scene when I pass a sign that reads, "Angola 14 miles." I straighten up and shift into my journalist mindset. *I'll treat this like one of my job assignments*, I think ridiculously.

I've done much research in the weeks and months leading up to today, as if it could ever prepare me for this visit. I surfed the Net, contacted the small museum on the outskirts of the prison property and tried to construct Angola in my mind. I needed a picture. Set on 18,000 acres in Northwest Louisiana, this maximum-security prison was once a slave plantation, named after the country in Africa from which the slaves who worked it had come. In the 1930s, prison life here was probably as close to slavery as a person could come. During that time, white-black racial tensions were at a boil. Each year one in every ten inmates was stabbed, and there was at least one murder a month. In the 60s, because of the number of inmate assaults, it was known as the bloodiest prison in the South, a virtual hellhole. Even as late as the 1980s, Angola's conditions were described as medieval, squalid and horrifying, so much so that hardened criminals broke down like babies upon hearing that they were being sent to Angola. There was a time when I couldn't help feeling satisfied that Nathan was sent to such a place. The documentary, *The Farm*, and the movies, *Dead Man Walking, Monster's Ball* and *The Green Mile* were all filmed or based on Angola. I'd watched each of them with much more than a passing interest. And how strange that the same Mississippi River running behind my grandfather's serene farm, over two hundred miles away, borders Angola on three sides, proving to be both a benefit and a burden. While its deadly current provides yet another barrier to contain five thousand of the most toughened criminals, repeated threats of flooding from hurricanes and heavy rains have plagued the prison throughout the years.

Highway 66 abruptly ends at the prison gate, where an overhead sign for Angola appears. Beyond it, a series of low-lying, single-story cement structures emerge from the horizon. With miles of rolled barbed-wire fencing, interspersed with guard towers on both sides of me, the damp and barren chill of outside air suddenly penetrates the inside of the car. I stop at the first checkpoint and give my name and proof of identification. I am on the list. I'm directed to wait in the adjacent parking lot for a man named Gary Young, the assistant warden, who will soon greet me in a prison van. I pull into a parking space, turn off the engine and listen at first to stillness. Through closed windows I silently scan the colorless terrain, when finally my eyes drift to the nearest guard tower. Inside, two uniformed men slowly move about their business. Just another day at work, perched between two extremes of those, like me, who come and go freely, and those who may never leave again. I wonder if Nathan Wolfe thought about this when he passed through this gate over twenty years ago. I wonder if I will be able to leave this place once I go in. I pull my jacket tighter across my body and secure my scarf around my neck. Then, I hear my breath, my heart, until they are deafening. I command my mind to shift from here to there, to yesterday in Florida, with my husband, my two daughters, my work, back to my familiar home and still waters.

Two
Phantom Limbs

Before dawn, the day of my departure, I sat at the kitchen table sipping coffee, looking out at the Loxahatchee River, waiting for the tangerine sun to inch its way over the mangroves lining the shoreline. Sitting calmly, meditating in the solitude of early morning, I waited for the alarm clocks to go off, shower doors to slam and the rhythm of the day to be set into motion. These sunrise mornings were not a daily ritual, but during times of stress or change they grounded me, silencing the voice of fear that commanded me for too much of my life.

I took my last sip of coffee as the first alarm clock sounded. Walking into my eldest daughter Sarah's room, I pushed the snooze button and climbed into bed with her, hugging her in the spoon position. Between the soft sheets, next to her warm body, I buried my nose in her neck, inhaling her familiar smell, feeling the smoothness of her skin. "Wake up, little Susie," I whispered.

"I'm not little Susie," she said groggily and with a little attitude.

"Oops, wrong bed then."

She tried to roll away from me, but I wouldn't let her until she opened one eye and groaned. Sarah, thirteen, independent and confident, was not at all interested in my sappy affections. But I still remembered her baby sweetness. Our early morning and late night chats in her bed kept me connected to her adolescent mind. Here in the darkness with just the two of us, the walls of her increasingly separate world disappeared.

When the second alarm sounded, I moved across the hall and climbed in with ten-year old Hannah, still sound asleep. I watched her for a moment, wondering to what far off and magical place she'd traveled. With my finger, I drew pictures on her back, just as my mother had done on mine. Waking her for school had never been simple. She finally turned over and wrapped her arms around me. With early morning cottonmouth she asked, "Is today the day you leave on your trip, Mommy?" I felt a pang. Leaving the girls had never been easy, but the prospect of this trip, in particular, daunted me. "I'll be back tomorrow night, sweetie, and you know I'll be calling." I hadn't told the girls much about my trip, other than I was writing a piece for work that required me to go to Louisiana. I was not ready to share the story of my mother's death for fear of worrying them, and not ready to have a convicted murderer enter their consciousness yet. Their innocent and safe world was a ruse, but it was also a gift I wanted them to have, at least for a little while. Eventually I would have to tell them, but not yet.

In the middle of the kitchen, hair disheveled, still in his boxers and T-shirt, Michael gave me a clumsy kiss, still half asleep. Even after fifteen years, his smooth dark Mediterranean skin and strong muscular build still invited me. "Morning," he said, reaching for a cup of coffee. After few slow sips, he leaned against the kitchen counter allowing the caffeine to sharpen his consciousness. With his eyes finally lingering on me, realizing that today was the day, I felt his silent lack of understanding, a quiet skepticism. Or perhaps it was my own insecurity. He'd tried to talk me out of this, worried for my safety, perhaps mental more than physical, and by extension the safety of our family. The tenuous symbiosis of marriage with predictable roles and mutual expectations from one another, especially in raising young children, was not foreign to us and perhaps now seemed more at risk than ever. How would this all affect me, and therefore him and the children?

He listened as I began to review the girls' schedules for the following days. I'd written it all down. Michael, a surgeon with a busy medical practice, had always been reasonable about adjusting his schedule as needed to look after the girls. "...and here's the number at Aunt Joy's, where I'll be tonight. I'm sure it'll be fine," I said, reassuring him and myself. "I'll have my cell with me the whole time."

After pony tails, lunches, longer-than-usual hugs, kisses, and a few tears from Hannah, they climbed into Michael's car. I closed the door behind them and let out a sigh. I hated leaving, but was unwilling to drag them into the blurry terrain where I was stepping. I looked at my watch.

Half asleep when the plane touched down in New Orleans, I dreamily remembered my annual summer trips to Louisiana as a child. Until the age of thirteen, I'd grown up in South America, living as an expatriate with my family because of my father's work as an international executive for IBM. Now, as the plane engines roared to a halt, I was transported back to these trips and the moment my mother stepped off the airplane onto the familiar terrain of her childhood. The heat rising from the black tarmac, the thick humid air beading up on our brows, she was instantly transformed into a southern belle, reverting to a deep southern drawl. "Hi y'all. We're finally he-ah. How y'all do-in'?" She screamed and waved with excitement as she ran into the tight embrace of her parents and three sisters. For her, it seemed an endless year of separation. Suddenly, she was not just my mother, but a celebrated international traveler, a star and the center of attention. My brother and I were happy enough to feel the warmth of her spotlight.

And here they were again. My three aunts, now more delicate in body frames with gentle lines around their eyes, yet impeccably dressed with hair and faces done up, were waiting for me at the gate. What an elegant trio. Aunt Frannie held my face in her hands, smiling through eyes welled up in tears, while Jessie and Joy took my bags. Fawning over me just as they had my mother so long ago, I was the star now, surrounded by their attentions.

We drove from the airport, through the French Quarter. The city smelled of trash and urine trapped in thick humidity. A prostitute stood on the corner of Canal and Poydras Streets in broad daylight. My neck stiffened with disdain for this seedy place, even before Hurricane Katrina, which would leave this city in ruins, with little hope for recovery. Even though I spent many summers and my last two years of high school in this city, except for my aunts, I hadn't missed this place at all.

13

From the French Quarter, we drove to Elysian Fields, a nicer suburb on the edge of Lake Ponchatrain, to the home of my Aunt Jessie, the oldest of the four sisters. She lived alone in a lovely one-story red brick colonial where I noticed black wrought-iron bars across the windows and gates across the doors.

"Are these new?" I asked as we pulled a few things from the trunk.

"Oh no, honey," said Aunt Frannie, the second oldest. "We all have them. The crime has gotten worse out here." My mother, Jeannette, nicknamed Nettie, had been third in line, and then there was Aunt Joy, the baby.

Just inside the door, a strong familiar smell engulfed me. "Mmmm," I exhaled. "Darlin', I put up a pot of your favorite," said Jessie, a wonderful cook. Within minutes, I was seated at the large kitchen table with a bowl of red beans and Andouille sausage over rice. "Now tell me all about Michael and the girls," insisted Joy. The three of them, my southern Auntie Mames, so similar in appearance and mannerisms to my mother, that even after twenty-four years, I felt her presence like a phantom limb, a vital missing piece from a body that could never be whole again. I looked at them and saw an age-enhanced photograph of who my mother might have been: the soft lines around her eyes, the camouflage of grey hair to golden flax and a shorter style, a more rounded frame, and weathered spotted hands baring the onset of arthritis, yet still finely manicured with red nails. Their voices and fragrances, too, were all subtle suggestions of her unfulfilled physical self.

At sunset, we moved outside to the enclosed red brick, ivy-coated courtyard. Joy and I gently rocked on the old porch swing while sipping sweet tea. Smoke swirled up as they took long slow drags on a cigarette they passed among them, while their reminiscent chatter reconstructed my mother's early life, before my father, brother and me.

"Joy, do you remember your high school dance, when Nettie gave up her shoes so you could go?" asked Jessie.

"Oh Lord, do I ever," whispered Frannie, nodding her head.

"What happened?" I asked, almost on cue.

Joy went on to say how poor they were, lucky to even have a pair of saddle oxfords for school. Even those were hand-me-downs. They wore them until they had holes on the bottoms and then my grandmother would get them re-soled. Jessie added that when their shoelaces broke, my grandmother would cut string to replace them, or when their toes started to poke through the front, they'd pass them down the line. Joy continued, "The only other shoes we owned were two pairs of black flats. Remember? We took turns sharing them between the four of us for church." Fortunately, Frannie and Jessie wore about the same size shoe as did my mother and Joy. On Sundays and other nice occasions, two of them would wear the dress shoes and the other two wore the saddle oxfords.

The cicadas filled the dense night air in perfect concert. The motion of the swing fell in rhythm as Jessie chimed in, "That's all Mama and Daddy could afford."

Once my mother and Aunt Joy were both invited to the same dance. They had a problem because they both shared the same pair of dress shoes. And on this occasion, saddle oxfords just wouldn't do. My mother insisted Joy wear the dress shoes, while she volunteered to work the registration table the entire night so she could at least attend the dance, but keep her saddle oxfords covered under a tablecloth.

"And of course, Joy accepted," taunted Frannie. "Joy, you certainly didn't put up much of an argument, as I recall."

"That's right. I danced while she watched, bless her heart," said Joy. "To this day, I feel badly that I didn't show enough gratitude to your mother. But that's how she was. The most generous and forgiving of us all." The conversation faded away momentarily.

"Your mother was a Tomboy when she was young," said Frannie, lightening it up and kicking off her shoes as she stretched her legs. I had never known this about my mother. "She was always outside helping Daddy with the farm, or sitting by the river with a fishing pole in her hand. She sure loved to fish."

"She'd come home with all that catfish and Mama would fry it up for dinner." Jessie leaned over for another sip of her sweet tea.

"She even used to catch crawfish and crabs in the drainage ditch out in front of the house. Mama cooked those too," said Joy. "We ate it all. I think it made Nettie feel good to know that she was helping out … and she was. Times sure were tight."

"Or maybe she just felt bad for poor Daddy, with five women in the house," said Jessie. "Lord knows, he needed a son."

Despite our closeness, there seemed so much I didn't know about my mother's life. Had she hidden all this from me? Or had I repressed the memories, my unconscious protecting me from some of the realities of her life? Or maybe she died when I was too young to understand the complexities of a woman. My memories of her were encapsulated in a separate dimension, only understood by youth and therefore irretrievable to me as a woman now. I listened intently to my aunts' stories, knowing full well they spoke of these times to help me fill in the gaps. I couldn't help but love these women, as they knit together an intricate shawl of warm memories, which as the evening wore on, they wrapped around me.

Finally, just before I was too tired to ask another question and they were too tired to tell, Aunt Joy asked, "Why are you going to Angola, baby girl? You have your own beautiful family now. Can't you just let it be? What's done is done."

I hugged her and whispered in her ear. "It's just something I have to do is all."

Three
Fire

My mother's life is a mosaic, created over time by my early memories, stories handed down by family members, old pictures, letters and documents. Each piece blends into another, seemingly sharpening my focus of her, but in truth, her story continues to evolve, even now.

One piece of the mosaic, an old black and white photograph of my mother, given to me by my aunt ten years after my mother was killed, sits plainly on my dresser inside an antique wooden frame. It's one of the few photographs I possess of her, as she never liked to be center stage. In it, my mother stands faded, but proudly, in her graduation dress, a white taffeta gown, trimmed with lace and covered buttons, sewn by my grandmother. Being photographed in an elegant dress was probably an extravagance for any of the Cutrera girls back then. With one hand gently poised on a railing and the other holding her rolled diploma at her side, she is elegant and serene before the camera, looking into the distance, as if pondering her hopeful future. Now frayed and yellowed, I keep the diploma, among other documents, like her death certificate, in an envelope in the bottom drawer of the same dresser.

Not revealed by the picture are events taking place in the background, beyond the perimeter of the frame, events immediately preceding and following the moment the photograph was taken, events that add a silent, but defining, dimension to everything that followed.

Prior to the graduation, everyone, especially my mother, the star of the evening, was rushing to make it to the auditorium at Promise Land Academy. Between negotiating who would wear which shoes and borrowing jewelry and dresses, the house was in a flurry. The table was set with Annie's Italian fig cookies laid out on doilies and a pitcher of sweet tea already brewed, all for the small gathering of family and friends who were to pay homage following the ceremony.

Although she was the third Cutrera daughter to complete this rite of passage, it was special nonetheless, as neither my grandmother, Annie, nor my grandfather, Papa Luke, had graduated from high school. In fact, Papa Luke never made it past the second grade. Because only Annie could read and write, she held a position of authority in the family, at least among her four daughters, who mostly feared her. Papa Luke, protector and redeemer, often stood between the girls and Annie, who alternatively used her kitchen spoons for cooking and discipline. "Oh come now, Annie," he'd try to reason on behalf of whichever daughter had crossed her, "leave the girl alone. She didn't mean no harm." Standing well over six feet tall (two feet taller than his petite and feisty wife), Papa Luke could usually talk her down from a snit or a rage and prevent a whooping if he was home. But Annie was her own kind of pillar, too, always making sure her four daughters were well dressed, fed and instilled with pride. "You're a Cutrera, after all," she'd say, as if they were the Kennedys.

Despite how poor they were, this was the Deep South, when even the poorest of white families employed black help. Annie had worked out an amicable arrangement with Beatriz (pronounced Be-átriz), a stout black woman who lived just up the river in Point la Hache with Isaac, her husband and a Baptist minister, and their seven children. Beatriz limped because one leg was shorter than the other and had teeth as white as cotton. Although the two families were probably equally poor, the Cutreras were, by Southern standards, better off by the mere color of their skin. Annie was "Miss Annie" to Beatriz, and Beatriz was just "Beatriz" to Annie.

Annie and Beatriz needed each other in practical ways. Beatriz came on Saturdays to help Annie and the girls clean their small two-bedroom house and help with harvesting, canning and pickling all of Papa Luke's cucumbers, tomatoes and vegetables from the garden. In return, Annie, a skilled seamstress, sewed clothes for Beatriz and her seven children. Her sewing skills kept her own family and Beatriz's well clothed, while bringing in a few extra dollars through alterations for wealthy women of the parish. If nothing else, Annie could be proud of the way her daughters dressed, particularly on special occasions such as a graduation. She did this for each of them, not only out of pride, but as her own gesture of love, as it wasn't her nature to show any physical affection or, God forbid, say, "I love you."

I conjure the scene just prior to the graduation and the photograph. "Hurry up y'all. We're gonna be late for the ceremony," Frannie hollered, while Jessie rummaged through their shared closet for a slip to wear. "We had to share everything, but we didn't mind. That's just how it was," my mother once told me. All four girls slept in the same room on a double sized bed, "spoon style … when one turned over, we all had to turn over." Additionally, they had no bathroom in the house, just an outhouse, which at night, always involved one sister keeping watch on the porch, while the other tiptoed lightly in her pajamas across the crushed shell drive, trying not to feel the sharp, broken edges against tender skin not yet hardened. "Are you watching me, are you watching me?" the one in the outhouse whispered loudly and fearfully into the darkness, while the other affirmed her watchful presence, until they were both safely back in the house – an outhouse buddy system. Between the pitch black of country night, the screeching cicadas, the rattlers and pythons my grandfather sometimes killed with his shovel, they had a well-substantiated fear of what lurked out there in the Bayou.

Joy stood in front of the small hallway mirror doing her hair, while my mother, humming, ironed her beautiful graduation dress in the kitchen. Jessie and Frannie continued dressing, while Annie, ready and in the yard, sealed the shed from those blasted raccoons that had on more than one occasion entered and knocked over her jars of preserved fruits and vegetables. Papa Luke was sitting behind the wheel of Bessie, their old Chevrolet, with the engine running … just trying, as usual, to stay out of the way.

The sisters eventually hurried down the stairs and into the car. My mother, like a young bride rushing to the church, was the last to pull the door of the house shut behind her. In the typical chaos of a family of six trying to make it to an event on time, one provident detail was forgotten. The iron. No one realized, especially my mother, that she forgot to turn it off and that this would shape not only her life, but also all of her family's for years to come.

By the end of the graduation ceremony, Wallace, a family friend and the local sheriff in Braithwaite, stood at the back of the auditorium looking for my grandfather, who hovered about a foot taller than everyone else. Finally spotting him, Wallace waved for him to come quickly, as my proud mother slipped off with her diploma to take the picture that would forever capture the event. My grandfather, grandmother, Jessie and Frannie rushed back to the house with Wallace, while Joy stayed back to wait for Nettie, happily unaware of their unfolding nightmare. At the click of the camera shutter, the family house was ablaze, with flames devouring and spewing their lives into the night. The photograph captured my mother's rite of passage from youthful naiveté into womanhood, permanently imprinting the event for posterity. It was the only picture salvaged and one of my few keepsakes from that time in her life.

When the family returned home, they were brought to their knees in front of the smoldering rubble. Nearly everything was destroyed except a few charred items covered in soot, one of which was a miniature porcelain tea set that belonged to my mother and now me. To make matters worse, my old world grandfather didn't believe in banks and stored all the family money under the mattress. So devastating was this fire that the family had to separate and live with different relatives for nearly a year.

Sometime after the fire, a terrible word surfaced. *Electroshock.* Following the fire, my mother fell into a deep depression. Although no one overtly blamed her, the fact remained that she had been the cause of the devastation and she could not forgive herself. Perhaps it would have been easier to hear outward accusations of her being so absentminded and thoughtless, rather than the family's silence. When she walked into a room where one or another family member was discussing any one of the hundred problems arising from the fire, they would change the subject or become silent. Although they may have been trying to spare her guilt, she inadvertently became the outsider. Of course on some level, they must have been silently angry and blamed her, but they also loved her. No amount of love could alleviate the weight of this guilt as it bore down on her, shackling her like a prisoner in her own mind. Had it been one of her sisters who left the iron on, bringing the family to ruin, she could have forgiven them immediately, but forgiving herself was another matter entirely. How easily she could forgive others, even her own murderer, as I later divined. But when it came to herself, she simply could not. For months, unable to eat or sleep, she barely spoke a word and cried constantly. The crisis of the fire then shifted to the crisis of Nettie unraveling. Day by day she grew worse, more gaunt and lifeless, almost zombie like. They were all exhausted from their loss, and no one knew what to do for her.

"Things were different back then, honey," my Aunt Joy told me years later on one of my visits as I looked at her wide-eyed across her kitchen table at first mention of the word. I had seen *One Flew Over the Cuckoo's Nest*, which ranked among the top most disturbing movies I'd ever seen. I cringed at the thought of my mother strapped on a table, electrodes connected to her head, convulsing at the flip of a switch. I could always count on Aunt Joy to answer my probing questions about my mother's past honestly, but tenderly. "They didn't have the same treatments and medications as they do today. The only thing they could offer her was electroshock therapy. No one wanted her to suffer this terrible guilt. It made her forget and she was able to go on with her life."

And forget she did. The only thing her sisters knew was that she went away for a week, to a hospital they were told. When she returned, she was calm, but frail and confused, as if part of her brain had been sealed off. Joy, who worshipped Nettie, took it upon herself to be her sister's keeper, playing "Do you remember?" games and trying to jog her memory, which had largely been wiped clean. When Nettie couldn't remember something, Joy would tell her stories, trying to implant her past, reassembling her identity, trying to make her whole again.

21

After the fire and my mother's "nervous breakdown," as it was called, family, friends and even strangers from the community came forward. A kindly stranger of means in the community eventually offered his large and empty house to the Cutreras for a period of time, until they could rebuild their own, this time with a bathroom inside. It took about two years to complete, but their new home, the one of *my* childhood summers, stood solidly for over fifty years, until Katrina.

Although my mother had loosely mentioned the fire, she never mentioned she caused it or spoke of her depression to me. I imagine that she quietly carried it within her. Had she not told me out of shame, as depression carries its stigma? Or perhaps she was like an amnesiac, unable to fully reconstruct her erased past. Like many things about my mother that seem cloaked in secrecy, I'm not sure, but it seems enough to know that the fire, while it left no visible mark on her, burned her deeply from the inside out.

Four
Water

My father, similar to my mother, had a defining childhood event for which he could not forgive himself. Like the moon orbiting the earth, it held him within a forcefield and fixed a trajectory for his future. For me, little else about his life could be wholly separated from it, although it too remained largely invisible and unspoken of for all the years that followed it.

In 1970, my father's job took us to Montevideo, Uruguay. For him, coming to this place as an adult, with my American mother, brother and me must have unearthed his childhood. It was his third foreign assignment with "Big Blue," IBM. But unlike the others, this place was not foreign to him, as he'd spent a decade of his youth here. He had roots embedded in this soil, a history with aunts, uncles, old neighbors and Jesuit school teachers who remained twenty years after he left.

One particular Saturday, my father took my mother, brother and me on a family outing to see the house where he'd lived as a boy in downtown Montevideo, minutes from where we were living. It was a modest concrete row house, nestled along the main drag of a congested street bordering the commercial district. We stepped off the street, past a gate and into a small courtyard, where there was an old mosaic-tiled fountain in the center. My father moved past us and up the stairs. He knocked on the front door, but no one answered. After a moment, he shifted his gaze to the dried-out fountain with faded and cracked mosaic tiles, where his face seemed to reflect inner echoes and dark shadows of a faraway place. Something in his eyes changed, evoking an unmistakable hint of longing and loss. "This is where it happened," he whispered. "Where Rodolfito drowned." While he and his two-year-old brother played outside one hot summer afternoon, soon after coming to this country, his brother slipped into the shallow fountain, perhaps hitting his head, or simply unable to regain his footing. My father had been one of five siblings, until there were only four. I had heard this story in fragments over time. It was a distant story told with little emotion, but in this moment I saw my father at age four going inside to tell his mother, "Mami, Rodolfito is sleeping in the fountain and won't wake up." My grandmother leapt down the stairs and into the fountain where her baby lay still, face down and blue. Her piercing screams of *"Madre de Diós, ayúdame, ayúdame!"* brought neighbors flooding into the courtyard, where she knelt drenched in water, cradling, sobbing and rocking him. My young father stood on the steps watching silently. Later that night, after the priest, relatives and close friends left, my grandfather broke the empty silence, asking my father a simple and indicting question, "Enriquito, why didn't you pull him out of the water?"

My father stood silently, confused and guilty for something he didn't understand. It had never occurred to him. Yet the die had been cast. As an adult, many years later, as he stood with us by the fountain, he was four again, still helpless, unsure of what he was supposed to do. And now, even more years later, in my own adult mind, I cannot help but embrace this little boy, for like my mother, he carried the guilt of ruining his family, and becoming an outsider, silently plagued by the nagging echo of *"If only I had ... "*

Through these childhood stories and others, I have become my parents' understudies, connecting the dots of their lifelines, a closed loop of sorts, where loss, pain and not forgiving recycle themselves from one generation to the next. As if it were a genetic trait, I wonder what I carry because of them and how I can break this cycle for myself.

After the death of his brother, his family moved from country to country, like mine, because of his father's work: from Cuba to Mexico to Argentina to Uruguay and then back to Cuba, before finally settling in the United States, where they all eventually became American citizens. My father grew to be a studious young man, educated by the Jesuits wherever they lived. Unlike his other three remaining siblings, he wanted to go to college and become an engineer. My grandfather, however, had other ideas. He was a stern and inventive man, determined to make a fortune by peddling a few patents on various and unusual gadgets, and wanted my father to step into the business once he was old enough. Being the first-born son of a traditional Cuban family earned my father inalienable responsibilities according to the constitution of his firmly ruling capitalist father. Against his father's wishes, however, my father became an engineer by working two jobs to pay tuition, and then went to work for someone else. This was a great betrayal (one of many sins tallied) by my grandfather's standards.

Feeling isolated by his father's angry grudge, my father sought comfort by marrying his first wife, a Cuban Catholic girl with silken black hair and porcelain white skin. She was the musically talented daughter of a prominent Cuban businessman and a future concert pianist. He brought her to the United States, where the family had finally escaped the stifling grip of Fidel Castro, who my father said was a lunatic. They fled to Minnesota, where it was twenty degrees below zero, taking only what fit into their suitcases. "Imagine that. A bunch of crazy, hot-blooded Cubans surviving the winters of Minnesota," he laughed.

Soon, under the pressure of his work and his young wife's passion for music, there wasn't enough to hold them together. "The only thing she ever loved was her music," he said bitterly. They lived separate lives, ultimately divorcing, but not before having three children, another family responsibility my father seemed unwilling to take on. And then, there was my mother, the American woman, "the whore," as my grandfather referred to her. Marrying her brought my father's disapproval rating to an all time high. This had been the final betrayal, which eventually earned my father a black sheep of the family status. My grandfather stopped speaking to him. "You and your illegitimate family are dead to me," he told my father.

"Divorce isn't permitted in the Catholic faith," my father, who had always been devout in theory, explained to me years later, as if my grandfather had no choice but to sever the relationship. Despite my grandfather's judgments and standards, my father never said an ugly word against the old man. Perhaps he felt he deserved his father's wrath for his many misdeeds, starting with the death of

Rodolfito. Respect was the cardinal rule, the unassailable postulate. "I was always afraid of my father. He ruled with an iron fist," my father would tell me. I understood just what he meant. "But he always had my respect."

Shortly after the visit to my father's childhood home in Montevideo and the fountain where Rodolfito drowned, my father announced that we would be traveling to Minnesota to meet my paternal grandparents for the first time. My grandfather was gravely ill. That we (my mother, brother and me) had never met my grandparents had not seemed strange to me for most of my childhood, perhaps because of the geographic distance between us, but all of the sudden I was uneasy about the upcoming trip, mostly about meeting my grandfather. Perhaps it was because I had never seen a dying person before, or more likely because of the deafening silence between my father and his father.

We traveled many hours and at great expense from Montevideo to Minneapolis. It took the whole night to fly from one continent to another. In those hours, I soared far above the world, suspended in time and place, safe in a cocoon. Weightless and free, I belonged to the skies. I loved the food, the blankets and the quiet steady roar of the engines, which muffled voices and dissolved worries. In the dark, the little overhead light above shined only on me. I drifted between worlds, where nothing else mattered. In the early morning, returning to earth and gravity, we touched down in Minneapolis on a bitter winter day, where the cold cut like a knife through flesh.

The halls of the hospital were antiseptic and bare. My shiny black patent leather Mary Jane shoes sparkled against the white linoleum, while the click clack of my heels made me feel as if I were Ginger Rogers. I secretly yearned for my father to step out of his serious character and into Fred Astaire's, making the wide corridor our stage, grabbing me by the waist and twirling me around, as he often did at home, all the way down the hall. He had taught me to dance starting when I was three, by placing a record on the turntable and holding my hands and body close to his as I placed my bare feet on his, mimicking his every step. Sometimes, he'd even place me on our large circular coffee table and dance me around it to the music. But there in the hospital, I felt the pull of my father's hand, his sweaty palm in mine and the tension in his tightly stiffened arm. Despite my temptation, I knew that dancing was out of the question. We seemed to be on a mission that day. My mother and brother walked alongside in silence. We were like soldiers marching, though not fully understanding the orders – only that we were to meet Abuelo, my father's father, for the first (and probably last) time.

When we finally arrived at the door of the hospital room, I looked inside and saw an old man lying prostrate and unshaven. Even this close to death, I could see he had been a handsome man, with remarkably similar features to my father. His sunken eyes, however, registered fear. The white sheets were tucked neatly around him, revealing how frail and shrunken he'd become. My father quietly hissed from his locked jaw, "Introduce yourselves. Tell him how happy you are to meet him." His firm hands in the middle of Stephen's and my backs, pushed us to the side of the bed. My mother stood quietly behind us. My father's desperation was palpable.

I wondered who initiated the visit, but cannot help but surmise now, in all likelihood, it was my father who made this final plea to break the code of silence. But his deep-rooted guilt and desire for approval or even just forgiveness, by a complete stranger to my brother, mother and me seemed a ridiculous attempt to reconcile at the eleventh hour. My grandfather met our gaze, nodding his head slightly, as if finally succumbing to his own war, too exhausted to fight anymore. To me, it barely seemed a look of acknowledgement, an empty, partial and belated gesture from a frightened old man. We left shortly afterward. My father, at first trying to be positive about the meeting, as if something had been granted, lapsed into another of his many stormy silences.

Only a few short days after we returned to Montevideo, the phone rang. My mother answered, and then quickly passed the phone to my father. Her eyes rested gently on him as he listened to the Spanish-speaking caller. Saying little in return and only in a whisper, moments later he hung up and walked silently into my parents' bedroom. My mother trailed behind him. I knew *El Viejo* had died. I do not remember any tears, ceremony or even much discussion regarding his passing, as if the grieving had happened long before.

While my parents' early lives were vastly different from one another, separated by class, continents and culture, they shared a common legacy of tragic loss and guilt, which seemed to define their lives and the true essence of their union. Both were irrevocably marked by catastrophic accidents, for which they felt responsible and not forgiven, either by others or themselves. They were two different elements, fire and water, yet they ignored the laws of nature while still drawing near to one another, as if trying to defy all odds. What mixture of genes, upbringing, emotions, social climate and education might have influenced my parents, or anyone for that matter, including Nathan Wolfe? Hadn't there been a time when they all had dreams of a more positive life?

Five
Angola
(2004)

Gary Young, the Assistant Warden, pulls up next to me in the prison parking lot in his white utility van labeled *Louisiana Correctional Facilities*. We both step out of our cars to introduce ourselves. He is a handsome, slender man, standing close to six feet tall, gracious and soft-spoken, with kind eyes and a discernable Southern accent. Not what I would expect from a prison warden at one of America's toughest maximum-security prisons. He asks if I've had lunch yet. I haven't. It's midday and my stomach is rumbling. I'm unsure if it's from hunger or nerves. Guiding me into the passenger seat of his van, he says, "Well, let's take care of that first."

My decision to visit Angola is not wholly explicable to others or me. Blind conviction has called me to arrange this visit, pay for an airline ticket and a rental car and drive four hours through rural and unfamiliar territory to visit the grave of a killer, a man I never met, and to learn about the place he spent most of his life after ruining mine. *At least I get a free lunch for my trouble*, I think.

Gary turns the van onto a gravel road stretching miles ahead and drives us to a small building called the Ranch House. It's a quaint gray house with white shutters and flowerpots in the windows; it does not fit the surrounding stark terrain. As we enter, Gary explains that this is where special visitors are served lunch by two inmates who have risen to a trustee level for "good behavior." I look at them, trying not to stare, and wonder what heinous crimes they have committed, how many lives, including their own, have they destroyed? They are an embodiment of Nathan Wolfe, as if these men are all the same, the worst of the worst: murderers, rapists, armed robbers, arsonists, all guilty of unforgivable acts. The litany of crimes committed by condemned men at Angola seems endless.

"Good behavior" implies reform. *Is that really possible in a place like this,* I wonder? *Even if it is, what difference does it make? Do these people deserve to be rewarded after what they've done? How can they be forgiven for what they have done to others? How can they forgive themselves for the death or destruction of another human being's life, even if unintentional?* In this moment, I feel upended and uncertain by questioning such things, things about which I have been so certain.

"Here you go, ma'am," says one of the trustee inmates, as he gently slides a plate of less than palatable, watered down rice, sausage and green beans in front of me. "Would you like sweet tea or water?" he asks. I can barely eat, yet I imagine this is probably the best food in the whole prison.

Over lunch, Gary describes the history of the prison, a talk I'm sure he's given hundreds of times. After being a slave plantation before the Civil War, it became a state-sanctioned prison for society's worst offenders, nicknamed "Alcatraz of the South," where gang violence, sexual slavery, disease and hopelessness prevailed.

"Sexual slavery?" I interrupt.

"Where one prisoner could own another for his use. Violent rapes weren't reported for threat of being raped again, or even killed. Most prisoners preferred death, until Burl Cain, the current warden, took over in 1995. We had a lot of suicides back then." Over time, Gary continues, Cain improved many of the conditions by giving the men a sense of purpose through paid jobs, education and faith. Even though inmates' sentences remain the same, Cain has given them some possibility of hope through a reward system and a religious-based concept called *Moral Redemption*. My curiosity piqued, I make a mental note to find out more about this later. Evidently, Cain is a strong Christian. Gary also tells me that Cain has an open door policy (within safety limitations) and does not shy away from the media. I suppose that's why I am allowed to be here.

I look past him and see signed photographs of Billy Bob Thornton, Barbara Walters and various celebrities on the wall. Angola, now somewhat of a historical and Hollywood landmark, has drawn many actors and celebrities as they act out or explore powerful stories of violence, guilt, forgiveness and redemption. Perhaps they began their tours here as well, maybe even sitting in my same chair, drinking from my same glass. I can't help but feel special in this way. I had simply requested a tour as a writer and a victim. Maybe they think I'm an up-and-coming Hollywood screenwriter or a best-selling author. Or maybe they're just trying to help people, like me, set things right.

Six
History Mystery

A few years after losing my mother, while I was still in college and on spring break, I visited my Aunt Joy at her home in Chalmette, Louisiana, not far from where my mother was killed. Even though I tried to steer clear of Louisiana and the black memory it now held, being at Aunt Joy's was a safe haven, the next best thing to home, when I had nowhere else to go. We had spent a solemn day going through boxes containing some of my mother's belongings, which were packed away after the murder and sale of her house. After we were done, we sat drinking sweet tea at her kitchen counter. The silence of the house invited me to ask, "How did my parents meet?" Their union had always been a mystery to me, and perhaps to them as well. How did I not know this story? I was becoming an archeologist on a quest for relics, uncovering the truth in fragments.

"Two years after the fire, your mama managed to scrape together enough money to go to secretarial school and get a job at Nichol Sulfur Company, where she met your father," she recounted. "They were both working there, about ten miles away from our rebuilt home in the country."

My mother, a delicately framed Southern woman of Italian descent with soft and rounded features, worked as a secretary for the president of the company. My father, who worked as a contract engineer at the plant, was well educated and strikingly handsome in an Omar Sharif kind of way, with a perfectly proportioned and defined bone structure and deep-set eyes. He was Latin and lonely, for he'd only recently divorced (or so he said) his first wife, the Cuban concert pianist, with whom he had three children.

"He was like a movie star," my Aunt Joy continued. "He charmed not only your mother, but the whole family. None of us knew much about him, but he was so handsome, intelligent and proper. And that accent! He asked me to be a chaperone for them on their very first date. Your mother seemed happy, which made all of us happy, too."

On their first date, my father arrived at her door with purple irises in one arm and a box of chocolates in the other. Standing there a moment, in his crisp oxford shirt, pressed trousers and wing tip shoes, he juggled his gifts so he could knock on the door. Jessie, Frannie and Joy peeked from behind the living room blinds at him. "Glory be! The Latin Rock Hudson has arrived!" teased Frannie. My mother hurried to finish readying herself in the back room. She brushed through her curls, carefully applied blush and eye shadow, sprayed perfume on her wrists and neck and checked herself one last time while taking a deep breath. It would be a few minutes anyway, as the family would fuss over him before she could make her grand entrance. Papa Luke, still in his janitor uniform, had just come in from work. He snuffed out his corncob pipe in order to greet Nettie's celebrity admirer. He was secretly skeptical and more protective, after all Nettie had been through. He had met plenty of his daughters' suitors, all good ol' Louisiana boys from up the road, but this one was different.

"It is my pleasure to meet you, Mr. Cutrera," said my father extending his hand. Papa Luke, a man of few words, returned the gesture in silence. Within seconds, the three sisters and my grandmother gathered around him. He handed the box of chocolates to my grandmother. "This is for you, Mrs. Cutrera."

"Oh my. Thank you . . .," She stumbled. "How do you pronounce your name?"

"Enrique," he said in his Spanish accent rolling the r. "But just call me Hank. It's easier."

"That's for sure," giggled Jessie.

"Nettie tells us you're from Cuba. How'd you make it all the way over here?" asked my grandmother. They had seldom met a foreigner.

"I was born in Cuba, but my father's work took us all over South America. I came to the United States for engineering school. I've been here for seven years now." No mention was made of his wife and three children.

34

When my mother entered, all eyes, especially my father's, focused on her. He handed her the irises. Their eyes met. It was a fait accompli.

Still sitting at the kitchen counter, Aunt Joy continued, "Your father turned the tide for your mother and we didn't want to ask too many questions, as she seemed to be getting better." However, after only a few months of knowing each other, my mother, quite abruptly, packed her bags one day and told her sisters and parents that she was following my father to White Plains, New York, where they planned to go to a justice of the peace, get married and where he would start a new job assignment with IBM. No longer willing to protect my father, Aunt Joy added, "They eloped, probably because things were complicated with his first wife. We always believed he was divorced when he met your mama."

"No wonder they never spoke about it," I murmured. It explained why I never heard about any magical moments of the first when and where, of how they just knew, of wedding bells and happy ever after. There were still so many unanswered questions.

The lines on the map faded in White Plains, where my father began his promising new career and my brother, Stephen, was born. My mother had always been good about staying in touch with family, but during this time, all communications were temporarily cut. "We were worried because we didn't know what was going on," Aunt Joy explained. "There was just silence for a very long time. Papa Luke wanted to send me up there to check on her, but we didn't have the money." Dates such as my brother Stephen's birthday, my father's divorce from his first wife and my parents' marriage were blurred. The geographic distance and lack of modern communication provided the smokescreen they seemed intent on maintaining.

Aunt Joy interrupted our conversation. "Wait a minute, sugar, I need to get something." When she returned from her den, she held a large manila envelope, worn around the edges. "You're old enough, honey," she said, as she placed it on the table in front of me. My mother's handwriting, forever recognizable with rounded cursive lettering and imprinted in my memory, read *Confidential* on the front. I ran my fingers softly over it, and then lifted it to my nose, hoping to sense her presence. Curious, but suddenly nervous about what was inside, I paused before unfastening the clip and pulling out a stack of documents. My aunt sat silent, hands folded in front of her, letting me review the papers. Among them were my brother's birth certificate and my parents' wedding license. The mystery was finally solved. My brother's birth certificate was dated May 12, 1958, three months prior to my parents' marriage certificate, dated July of 1958. In all likelihood and the best we can figure, she became pregnant in Louisiana and fled to White Plains to have my brother and wait for my father's divorce from his first wife to become final before she and my father could marry.

I felt lightheaded and displaced all of the sudden, as if I were a plant being uprooted. The foundation upon which my family was created was based on secrets, shame and lies, suppressed, as if it could be erased, denied or forgotten. How strange that my mother filed these documents away, but did not destroy them. *Did she want me to eventually find out? If so, when? Did she think I would love her less because she made a mistake?* As if she were an accomplice to a shameful crime, she carried this all her life. She was the person I'd felt closest to the world, yet I felt all of the sudden as if I did not know her at all . . . until now. Until too late. A wave of exhaustion moved through me. I wanted to go to bed.

"The next time we heard from your mama was when you were born. She sent some pictures and told us that all four of y'all were moving to Puerto Rico," Aunt Joy finally added. This was the first of several places in Latin and South America where IBM sent us as expatriates. It was beginning to look like a rags to riches story for my mother. The rapid ascent of my father's international career must have been thrilling in many ways: promotions, titles, first class international travel, fine dining, entertainment, clothing and generous expense accounts. Yet I can't help but wonder how my father so easily reconciled leaving his three other young children behind, or how he divided one life from another. He bore no outward trace of guilt for leaving them, as if they didn't exist.

Seven
Culture Clash

For my mother, a new husband, the birth of two children and relocation to a new continent, all within three years of meeting my father were no small changes for a young Southern country girl from the bayou, who had grown up with an outhouse. Her desire to please him, however, was greater than her fear of the unknown or her inability to assimilate into such a culturally different world.

My father, who had spent his childhood in Central and South America among servants, couldn't understand my mother's discomfort managing live–in servants. Beatriz had been like a friend to the Cutreras. My mother disliked giving orders, especially since she couldn't make herself understood in Spanish. My father wanted her to become more proficient. Because of our age, my brother and I were able to master a second language, but my mother couldn't manage it. My father demanded that my mother learn to delegate, to behave more like an employer and not a friend.

We moved to Mexico, into a nice neighborhood called Chapultepec, a suburb of Mexico City, near my father's office. Like everyone else around us, we had servants, one hired for the upstairs and one for the downstairs. Francesca and Leonora were two young women who lived with us Monday through Friday, in a small building behind our house, a two-bedroom structure made of unpainted cement block with spare comforts. Leonora was short and stout with long black hair as thick as a horse's mane, always plaited, and a gentle smile that rested naturally on her round broad face. Francesca was more petite, thin-framed and less jovial, with deep set eyes and pointed features that seemed to suggest an intensity and perhaps a darker story or harder road than her partner. On the weekends they took a two-hour bus ride home to their small village, to be with their husband, boyfriend and families.

One Friday, Leonora and Francesca missed the last bus of the day. "We'll drive them tomorrow morning, so they can see their families," my mother insisted. It was two hours to their little town of Toluca. "It'll be like a field trip," she said. My father agreed to join us, because my mother was unaccustomed to driving in a foreign country, where the *banditos* and *policia* were governed by equal degrees of lawlessness. An American woman driving the Mexican countryside with two children and two servants was an invitation for a problem.

We set out early in the morning in our Ford LTD, with my parents in the front seat and me and my brother squeezed in back with Francesca and Leonora. While Stephen sat engrossed with his face behind a book, I sat happily, but also awkwardly, between the two women, closer than I'd ever been to them before. The skin of our arms and legs pressed up against one another and I could smell the natural oil from their hair, as if we were one body. Unsure of myself, I acted giddily, mostly out of the uncomfortable notion that we had crossed some invisible boundary between us, exactly where I could not say. Too young to understand, I was confused between my mother and father's conflicting stances on class and culture, feeling sandwiched between two worlds. *How was I any different than Leonora and Francesca, and why had I been born into my life and not theirs?* It was the first of many times I'd encounter such extremes as an expatriate, as if humanity could be so easily subdivided. Perhaps it was a primer for my future meeting with Nathan Wolfe, my nemesis and opposite.

We all looked out the window, as the landscape slowly gave way from tall city buildings and organized streets with roundabouts of famous Mexican figures, to low-lying cement block structures with pot-holed streets and barefooted children sitting amidst garbage on blankets, begging with outstretched hands. Eventually, the concrete road turned to gravel and the horizon became barren brush. Along the road, two women, sisters perhaps, were selling dead iguanas, holding them from head to tail, so cars passing by could see. "What do they do with them?" I asked Leonora in Spanish. "We eat them," she replied. My stomach flip-flopped. Further on, an old man carried two plastic jugs of water balanced on a pole across his back, while a younger boy of about my age walked alongside him doing the same.

Scattered along the road were emaciated stray dogs, a few even dead, off to the side. The dirt from the road coursed through our open windows leaving a layer of grit throughout the car. My father asked us to roll them up so he could put on the air-conditioning.

In our travels, my parents never failed to highlight the dichotomy between worlds and our good fortune, but entering Francesca and Leonora's world now brought it into sharper focus. We only ever saw them in our home, with neatly pressed uniforms and nice shoes, which my parents made sure they had.

After about two hours, Leonora directed us to the end of a dirt path, explaining that the car could not be driven any further. All we could see ahead were what looked like a conglomeration of haphazardly constructed shanties made of corrugated metal, cement blocks and scrap wood, with dirt floors, no electricity or plumbing. A strong wind or heavy rain could easily level this neighborhood, and probably had many times before. We said goodbye and let them out. My mother, brother and I craned our necks to watch them walk off, unable to turn our eyes away, as my father spun the car around, flipped on the radio and happily drove us home.

By comparison, their living quarters behind our home were a vast improvement over their own homes in Toluca. After our family field trip, however, when my father was at work, I saw my mother from my second story bedroom window, sneaking extra blankets, lamps, furniture and clothing into their living quarters. I knew enough not to mention it to my father.

Neither Francesca nor Leonora spoke English, but my father spoke perfect Spanish with them. My father, whose full name was Enrique Angel Gutierrez Marbán, spoke English fluently, but with a thick Spanish accent, saying "poodle" instead of "puddle," ending many of his statements by asking "no?" "The garden is beautiful, no?" Yet, except for certain words or when someone else commented on it, I didn't notice my father's accent. Although I didn't think of him as Spanish and respected his pride in being an American citizen, I was vaguely aware of something separating him from us, his American-born family.

On the occasion of her thirtieth birthday, my father gave my mother a small sterling silver bell with a handle. He placed it at the center of the dining room table. Its jingle was much like that of holy bells used to call attention to the consecration of sacraments during the Catholic mass we attended every Sunday. My father, the omnipotent master of his domain, wanted my mother to use the bell during dinners to call Leonora from the kitchen for mango jam and bread or to clear the china plates. But it sat in the center of the table, mostly untouched, except when my father insisted.

"Ring the bell. What do you think I pay her for?" he said, slamming his fist upon the table.

"She does other things," my mother said quietly. "It's demeaning to her. I'll get it myself."

Exasperated, he grabbed the bell, ringing it loudly, until Leonora appeared, confused by his tense and emphatic tone. "Leonora, Señora would like you to bring her a fork."

My mother sat silently, staring blank-faced in a different direction.

"Si, señor," Leonora said, bowing her head, clasping her hands in front of her white starched apron and black uniform and backing out of the room before scurrying off to the kitchen.

Predictably, a loud and firm pontification about South American class structure and customs followed, continuing until we were all sufficiently disinterested in our food and excused from the table. Later, while undressing for bed, I imagined Francesca and Leonora must have spoken quietly between themselves, commenting about my father's dark moods and my parents' arguments, like buried mines between two foreign lands.

Not long afterward, when my mother noticed forks, knives, plates and glasses were disappearing one by one from our house, she tried to ignore it. When clothing and finer linens started vanishing, it began to gnaw at her. When it became cash and jewelry, she realized she had to do something. One day, I was home alone with Francesca, the upstairs servant. I was playing quietly with my Barbie dolls -- an impressive collection I had amassed from visitors from the states who asked what special gifts they could bring us. Once again, from my open bedroom window above the drive way, I witnessed Francesca and her boyfriend, who had come from their village, loading bags and boxes of our belongings, even small pieces of furniture, into the back of a run-down borrowed truck. I perched closer to the window on my knees to listen to their hushed and hurried words.

"Did you get the boy's blazer and sneakers?" I heard him ask Francesca. Francesca's boyfriend was not much bigger than my brother, so all of his clothes fit, which explained why more and more of my brother's clothing had been missing in recent weeks.

"Yes, and here, I'll help you with this box. It's heavy," she said. "It has the señora's extra plates. She never uses them."

I leaned a little closer, looking over the ledge to get a better view. But in a split second, I pulled back, unsure if she had seen me out of the corner of her eye. The boyfriend drove off hurriedly. When I heard Francesca coming up the stairs, I busied myself again with my dolls. She stopped under my doorway, staring at me for a moment. "My boyfriend came to pick up some things that your mother *gave* me."

"That's good," I said, pretending everything was fine, unsure of how else to respond.

However, when my mother returned a few hours later, I told her, "Mom, Francesca's boyfriend came to pick up all those boxes, bags and furniture you gave her."

"What are you talking about?" She asked wide-eyed, then rummaged through the house to see what was missing.

In her broken Spanish, I listened to her confront Francesca, who vehemently denied everything, accusing me of not liking her and of being a liar. When my father came home from work, my mother ultimately had no alternative but to tell him, carefully omitting much of what had transpired up to that day. Immediately after, I heard him fire Francesca. My father, beyond furious, paced back and forth in front of my mother, fists clenched behind his back, as she sat on the couch, silently submitting to his loud criticisms of her not having control over the servants, of being incompetent as first lady of the house.

Later that night, after he retreated into his angry silence, my mother came into my darkened room to kiss me goodnight. Knowing I was unsettled, even frightened, by what had transpired throughout the day and night, she lay next to me running her fingers through my hair, asking about my latest school project and my friend's birthday party, trying to diffuse my worry. "Finally," she whispered, "If Francesca needed those things badly enough to steal them, then she should have them. Remember where they live."

"Dad is so angry, though," I added, as if she hadn't noticed.

"That's his choice," she said calmly. "It's alright, honey."

I wasn't so sure.

A few weeks later, my parents were hosting a dinner party for my father's Latin business acquaintances and friends. Up in my parents' room, as always, I sat and talked with my mother while watching her dress. I helped her zip up the back of her gown, decide between two pairs of shoes and fasten her jewelry. I shared my friend problems and challenges at school. "And then what did you say?" she'd ask, again and again, truly interested. And of course I rambled on, spilling it all out, until it was time for her to join my father. In addition to her wise words, her finishing signature touch was always a spray of Chanel #5 at the nape of her neck and on her wrists. The rich fragrance of cinnamon and deep woods wafted through every cell in my body, transporting me to somewhere near nirvana. Best of all, afterward, she'd rub her wrist against mine to share, but not to overpower me. I believed if I ever lost her, even if all my other senses failed me, I could always rely on this scent to bring me back to her.

Wanting to make the proper impression and please my father, my mother wore her hair in an elegant French twist, accented by the delicate pearl-drop necklace and earrings that he had given her. Her pink painted nails matched her flowered chiffon dress, which gently swayed from side to side as she glided across the floor in her high-heeled sandals. To me, she looked like she stepped out of a glamour magazine to entertain famous international dignitaries.

Guests were invited for eight o'clock. She had planned an exquisite dinner, perfectly timed for nine o'clock. This would have allowed for cocktails, hors d'oeuvres and chatting, despite the fact that she understood little of what they were saying. By nine-thirty, no one had even arrived, and I sat in my pajamas at the top of the circular stairs, my favorite observation perch, waiting for people to show up. When my mother inquired, my father snapped, "Haven't you figured out that we dine later here? It's our (including himself now) custom. Relax!" By ten, when the roast was dried out and the vegetables overcooked, the doorbell rang. By ten-thirty, all of the guests had arrived. From the stairs I watched my father and the guests in full swing, speaking nothing but Spanish, while my mother, exhausted and subdued, smiling fixedly, distantly, trying to be the good wife, the Latin wife my father now seemed to want.

Yet despite her discomfort, she transcended her cultural naiveté, often through self-deprecating humor and good will. When a washing machine that was supposed to be delivered on a particular Tuesday wasn't, she called to speak with the store manager who understood no English whatsoever. As she rambled, he kept asking *Mande?* (a Mexican term for "what?"), which she only understood to be *Monday?* She insisted endlessly with him for a faster delivery than the following week, but to no avail, for all had been lost in translation. Later, when she discovered her blunder, we had a good laugh with friends, family … and even my father.

Through a combination of good nature and sheer tenacity, she managed to help propel my father's career to the next level, earning him yet another promotion and transfer to another country, even deeper into foreign terrain.

Eight
Family Portrait

In my late thirties, I spent a Sunday afternoon cleaning out a storage closet, trying to make space for my daughter's baby furniture. I was unwilling to part with it just yet, as Michael and I were still discussing the possibility of a third child. In the very back of the closet, buried behind boxes containing my childhood doll collection, university diplomas, wedding photos and my mother's porcelain keepsake figurines, I came upon something long forgotten. A large object wrapped in thick cloth. I gently removed the dark wrapping one layer at a time and stood back to fully view a portrait of my childhood family. I gazed at this frozen scene for a long time, remembering the moment in Montevideo, Uruguay, 1970, when I was ten years old. I examined the expressions on each of the faces.

In this portrait, my father sits sternly at the head of the dining room table, rigid and business-like, my mother to his left, my brother to his right, both looking reverently and intently at him. A slight coral-colored smile is fixed on my mother's face. My younger self, frozen in paint, reveals a ten-year-old girl in the throes of something undefined. My face, framed by wavy chestnut colored hair pulled back in loose pigtails, seems sweet, but forlorn. Or perhaps worried. I stand at my mother's side, with one hand on her shoulder, the other resting on the table with her hand reaching over, holding mine. My eyes are cast downward, solemnly, staring at the table. Even the table poses: a lace tablecloth with small embroidered yellow flowers, fine bone china plates, a small silver bell, delicate flowers in a vase, a bottle of red wine with two crystal glasses, a loaf of bread and some fruit.

A well-known Uruguayan artist, Osvaldo Leite, was commissioned by my father to paint the large oil portrait to fit perfectly on the living room wall. When we first met Señor Leite, a slight man with a mustache and goatee, he surveyed our family, his subjects, intently, as if trying to capture our essence. My father insisted we pose in the dining room, sitting at the large Spanish rustic wooden table. Señor Leite preferred live subjects. So, over several days and many hours, we posed in a painfully still position. I grew weary from the terse ventriloquist conversations in which, my father, between fixed lips, threatened to erupt if any of us complained. When the painting was finally framed and hung, friends commented on what a unique and magnificent piece it was and what a handsome family we were.

This family rendering survived many moves and when it finally came into my possession as an adult, I left it wrapped and stored for safekeeping, unwilling to think too much about it. But on this Sunday afternoon, almost three decades after it was painted, gazing at this seemingly perfect scene, I still felt the subtle tension among us, captured in the still shadows of oil on canvas. I was a voyeur, peering at a scene of strangers, yet knowing them more intimately than anyone else in the world.

~~~

At this table in the portrait, my parents sat one Sunday morning over breakfast while I played upstairs in my room, pretending to have a tea party with my dolls. Stephen, always behind a book, was in the library. The sequence of the sounds I heard came quickly: first a single and loud *POP*, then shattering glass and then my mother's scream. I stopped what I was doing and ran downstairs to see what happened. My feet, not carrying me fast enough, stumbled, as I held the railing to keep from falling. I arrived at the closed dining room door breathless, my heart pounding. As I opened it, my father screamed, "STAND CLEAR OF THE WINDOW" - the window that was no longer there, but strewn all over the room in pieces. My mother sat in the corner of the room, away from the window, shaking uncontrollably, while holding a napkin to her forearm. My father moved past me quickly to the nearest telephone in the library. Frantically dialing, I then heard him speaking Spanish to someone, perhaps the police. Desperate to get to my mother, but afraid to walk in front of the window, I stood frozen.

Within a few minutes I realized that a bullet had passed within six inches of my mother's temple and lodged in the opposite side of the dining room in the wall, but not before shattering the window, a piece of which cut her forearm.

Luis, our groundskeeper and guard, went in and out of the room, while I sat rigidly watching. His hand rested upon a pistol that was holstered around his waist. "You and your brother are not to go outside for the rest of the afternoon," my mother commanded, barely stifling back tears. It sickened me to see my mother so upset, to think that she might have been hurt, or even worse, killed. Although I had always worried about it before, I knew now, beyond a shadow of a doubt, that I could lose my mother. This foreboding knowledge planted itself deep within my belly. As if her killer would always remain a ghost, it did not matter whether it was this anonymous shooter or Nathan Wolfe, she would eventually be taken from me. But she had narrowly escaped fate's first attempt.

My parents gathered my brother and me into the living room for a family summit. While we sat on the couch, my father paced from side to side, hands clasped behind his erect back. "It appears a pellet from a BB gun, or something like that, has gone through the window where your mother was standing." I could tell by the way she was still shaking that it wasn't a BB gun. "It was probably just some kids fooling around, a prank or something. Everything is under control, though. The American Embassy has sent some men over to look around and the police are here as well." Holding my doll tightly, I saw strange men, some in police uniforms and some in black suits, walking around our front yard and house. They carried machine guns, which they pointed at bushes in our beautifully landscaped garden, at the shed and all around the outside of the house.

That night, and for several weeks, I was too frightened to sleep in my room. At first I slept in my parents' room, but was afraid of the gun under my father's pillow. Then, for many nights after, I slept in my brother's room. I had nightmares about a secret witch's door under my bed and thought I saw a ghost. The rest of the house slept, or so I thought, while I lay awake imagining there were Martians in the backyard, coming to take my mother away. When I related my troubling nightmares to my parents, my father laughed at me, saying, "you have an overactive imagination." My mother tried to assure me, embracing me. "Everything is fine, honey." But she wasn't good at lying. She seemed preoccupied and busy all the time.

The week after the bullet, IBM provided us with heightened security. Every school morning, at the same table in the portrait, my brother, Stephen and I ate our cereal, while my mother bustled around in her robe, packing lunch bags. She urged us to hurry, as our ride waited. By 7:00 a.m. a man in green knocked on the front door. He always wore the same outfit with a machine gun slung over his shoulder like a purse. I kissed my mother good-bye as I climbed into the blue van with my brother and the man in green, who sat in front with a driver. My mother stood in the doorway, thin-lipped and rigid. As the car pulled away, I turned to look at her. Her eyes betrayed her. She looked like a mother standing by the operating room door after handing off her baby to the doctor performing open-heart surgery. I saw her watching us all the way down Lido Street until we turned onto Las Ramblas.

In the back seat of the van, Stephen started our silent game. He nonchalantly bumped my knee. I poked his arm. He waited a moment, pretended to yawn and stretched his arms while casually brushing his hand against my hair. I waited, turned abruptly to point out a make believe something on the street, while my foot gently tapped his. The men in front sat stone-faced, the machine-gun between them, oblivious to our childish antics, or perhaps our unconscious counterpoint to the threat around us. This continued until we stopped to pick up other children. I touched him last, silently gloating in my victory. As we arrived at school we said *muchas gracias* to the driver and the man in green before immediately entering the building.

Everyone dressed in proper uniforms at The British School. Girls wore starched white blouses under stiff pleated forest green jumpers with neckties, which I thought was ridiculous. Boys wore blazers, neckties and khaki pants. My fifth-grade teacher, Mr. Jarman, a tall round man who spoke with a soft British voice calling pants "trousers" and cigarettes "fags," seemed to like me, probably because I had learned to be quiet and obedient in the six schools I'd attended in ten years. I followed the rules, unlike George Wright, a tall thin boy with freckles and wavy red hair whom I secretly called

George Wrong because he was always in trouble. Mr. Jarman frequently made him put his hands on the desk while he rapped his knuckles with a wooden ruler, penance for lifting a girl's jumper or for putting erasers up his nose. I was terrified of having my knuckles rapped.

During recess, I always looked for my best friend, Anne Granieri, an American expatriate like me. Her father worked with mine and our mothers were best friends. Although we'd known each other for only a few months, we were drawn together by our many moves, our mutual lack of enduring points of reference. We were members of the same tribe. We sat elbow to elbow at the lunch table, eating our peanut butter-and-jelly sandwiches. Afterward, we played four square or Chinese jump rope on the playground. Other girls, who came from many different places, joined in. Some came from Montevideo, some from England, some from the nearby Falkland Islands. There were only a few from America. North America, that is. The girls from Montevideo always reminded me they came from America as well ... South America. When the bell rang at three in the afternoon, the man in green waited for us. My brother and our other friends from the United States got into the van to go home.

Even though other children were going to school unprotected on buses, riding their bikes or even walking, it became routine going to school with the man carrying a machine gun. All the American expatriate kids did it now.

In the portrait, I focused in on my father, sitting at the head of the table so handsome and commanding. His black-framed glasses lent an even greater air of sophistication to his chiseled features. The prototypical conservative IBMer, with a Latin American flair, I mostly remember him in dark-colored suits, starched white collared shirts, subdued printed ties and wing-tipped shoes. He was a true Brooks Brothers company man, with a razor sharp sense of humor that most people thought hilarious. Acquaintances, mostly female, commented to my mother, "Enrique is so gregarious and charming. How do you stand it?"

"Oh, I manage." she'd say, flatly.

On Saturdays, however, when my father was more relaxed, he'd return from horseback riding at the Polo Club around midday wearing his jodhpurs and English riding boots. He'd stand erect in the center of our garden, surrounded by a tall wall protecting our home and property. Like landscaping of some regal mansion or estate, he inspected the perfectly trimmed bushes with small white stones bordering expansive and colorful flowerbeds, brimming with every variety of indigenous plant or flower.

With his riding crop and velvet helmet tucked under folded arms, he'd speak with Luis, the Uruguayan gardener and guard -- a large, partially bald man with long side burns who lived in our home with his wife, Marta. Luis tended to the outside and Marta the inside. Every few days, he picked flowers from the garden so Marta could adorn the inside of the house, always filling the pastel vase at the center of the dinner table. The smell of sweet fragrant gardenias and pungent daisies wafted beyond the vase and dining room into adjoining rooms, always subtly present as I moved through our home.

Whenever I played in the garden, Luis was nearby, sweat beading upon his brow, as he worked or planted. He wore a pistol strapped to his waist. I often played there with my German friend and neighbor, Sarah. Her father, Gunter, worked with mine at IBM. One of our favorite things to do was build forts out of old cardboard boxes. After we built them, we'd sit in them for hours, having lunch, talking, and playing games. Once, we even built one for my small white rabbit, Sam. Inside this small floppy house we placed carrots to lure him in. But Sam didn't trust us, probably fearing the house would collapse on him if he entered. He looked at the carrot inside the house with a laser beam stare, but refused to move. He stood paralyzed and confused, as if weighing the benefit of the carrot against the cost of being crushed. Finally, we pulled the carrot out and fed it to him. We played together on most weekends, always at my house, behind the large gates, with Luis working in our beautiful garden, never far from us.

Inside the house, Marta, a petite woman with a slight limp from childhood polio, worked hard to navigate between my mother and father's different styles. Marta offered to do the cooking, but my mother often preferred to do it herself. Occasionally they'd work side by side in the kitchen, but Marta was mostly relegated to cleaning the house, laundry and sewing.

Late one night about three weeks after the bullet missed my mother, the phone rang. In a dream state, my brother and I were taken from our beds and put into a van by more men with guns. My mother held me tight, cradling me in her arms, as we were driven to another location across town. I felt my mother's heart beating fast. I heard my father speaking Spanish quietly to the driver, but loud enough so that I heard him say, "bomba." It was only the next morning when I woke up on a couch in the American Embassy that I realized it was not a dream. My father tried to explain. "A man called our house last night and told us that we should sleep here. It was a false alarm. They've checked it out. Everything is perfectly fine. We're going home soon." I remembered the word "bomba." I imagined an explosion blowing the roof off our house. I worried about my rabbit Sam, who was left behind, and hoped he was safe.

At the dining room table the next evening, my father announced that we were getting a new dog. My brother and I were thrilled. This was what our family needed, I thought. A puppy would make things better. That weekend, a full-grown, sixty-five-pound German Shepherd arrived. We were summoned to the backyard for a demonstration. Holding a large stick wrapped in thick fabric and dipped in the blood of raw beef, a man said the word "Ojo," which means eye. Showing his pointy fangs, the dog growled from deep within his throat. When the man said, "Ataque," the dog leapt and sunk his teeth into the fabric, swinging the stick from side to side. The man held on to the stick while the dog tried to tear the fabric. When he said, "Bajo," the dog stopped. My brother and I stood there wide-eyed and stunned. "This is our new puppy?" I thought. My father told us that he was a pet *and* a guard dog, and that IBM had bought one for each of their expatriate families living in Montevideo. We were to learn these commands. He named the dog "Casique," which meant chief.

A week after Casique arrived, I invited my three friends, Anne, Jill and Sarah to my twelfth birthday party. It was a go-go-girl party, where we wore mini-skirts and boots. We played with Barbie dolls until my mother called us for ice cream and banana cake, served on a card table on the back porch. There were balloons, music, presents. We laughed and talked and after the cake, Anne suggested we play tag. I was it, so I chased my friends all over the backyard. Casique, after licking up the crumbs from under the table, joined in the chase. My friends stopped running, but I kept going. Jill, Anne and Sarah were frozen, watching as Casique chased me around the tree. It was no longer a game, as my heart quickened and chest tightened. I started to scream, calling for help. My mother watched frantically from the kitchen window before running outside, but Casique had already latched onto my arm, like the fabric on the stick. Luis came running as well. He hit the dog with a metal pole and dragged him away. My mother quickly wrapped my arm in a white towel and maneuvered us into the back seat of the car. Luis took the wheel after locking Casique inside the gardener's shed. The pounding of torn flesh, the sight of blood all over my shirt and miniskirt and the jarring bumps and turns through side streets of Montevideo on our way to the hospital shook everything loose in my head. I only remember that after stitches and shots we returned home to recount the story for my father, who had just returned home from Buenos Aires on a business trip. He suggested we keep a closer eye on Casique.

My parents fought more often now. Behind closed doors one night, I heard my mother say to my father, "We can't live like this anymore. It's not safe."

"Don't be ridiculous, we have guards and a dog. What are you worried about?" he said.

On what would prove our last Christmas in Montevideo, my mother, brother and I anxiously waited inside another of my father's increasingly angry silences. Living south of the equator, where seasons were opposite of North America's, seemed strange, as Christmas would fall during summer. And if that wasn't different enough, gifts weren't exchanged until January sixth, Three Kings Day. My parents argued over this. It began with her pleading, "why not let them follow the tradition they're accustomed to, where they open their gifts on Christmas like all their friends, and we'll hold a few gifts back for Three Kings Day." But he said, "When in Rome, we do as the Romans. The children need to follow *my* custom for a change." Unsure of which way the storm would blow or who would be the next target of his discontent, I kept silent, wishing the holidays were over.

In the early evening, only a week after Three Kings Day, I was laying on the floor doing homework in the living room. My parents sat across from each other reading. My brother was building a model airplane we had bought in the States. The smell of glue was noxious. On the television, I heard the wail of police sirens. They were the two-tone international sirens, not the American sirens with one long continuous whirling tone. We all stopped to watch. The announcer spoke about a man named Dan Mitrione, an American expatriate businessman, working internationally like my father. He had been kidnapped by a left-wing terrorist group called the Tupamaros. The police were searching for him. After they showed a photograph of him, his wife stood behind a microphone, crying, pleading in English for his release. The announcer translated what she was saying into Spanish. Pictures of Dan Mitrione were all over the television and newspaper for days to come.

"What's this about?" I asked my father, who looked serious as he turned away from the television.

"The Tupamaros are revolutionaries who don't want American business in Montevideo. They're trying to scare us into leaving, so they're using this man as an example, to scare us away."

"Will they hurt him?" I asked. What I really wanted to ask was, "Will they hurt us?"

"Of course not. They just want to make a point," he said. But I wasn't convinced. He must have seen my large eyes and tight lips. "They're not interested in people like us," he said. I was silent, wondering why then did we have Casique, guns and guards.

By the end of the week, Dan Mitrione was found with a bullet in his head, wrapped in a rug inside the trunk of a car parked in downtown Montevideo. School was cancelled for the American children. My mother, brother and I stayed at home with Marta, Luis and Casique. My father went to work, but at odd hours.

Eavesdropping from outside her room, I heard my mother speak to my grandmother by telephone. "He's finally agreed to put in for a transfer. It's just a matter of time. We're fine, Mama. Really."

Within a few weeks we learned that Dan Mitrione, an undercover CIA agent, had been sent by the U.S. government to intercept the Tupamaros. Instead, they intercepted him. The U.S. government promised to take action against the Tupamaros, but first they asked all non-essential employed Americans and their families, including us, to leave the country.

Finally, three months after my mother's close call with the bullet, all the heightened security, our midnight visit to the embassy and the death of Mitrione, my father received notice of a transfer. He delivered the news of our move in the worst possible manner. While sitting at the same dinner table in the portrait, one night, my father insisted we play a game that he invented. Starting with him, each person went around the table saying what everyone else could do to improve him or herself. "You could lose some weight and learn to speak Spanish," he said to my mother, as if she hadn't already tried. "And you," he said to me, "should cry less and not defend your mother so much. You act like a *chupamedia*," a slang term for something akin to ass-kisser. My brother's constructive advice followed, "try to be more athletic so people don't think you're a sissy." Unfortunately, no one else got a turn, because after he was done, I was already crying, my mother upset and my brother asking to be excused because of his recurring dinnertime stomach aches. The game ended with my father becoming irate at our lack of gratitude for his helpful comments, slamming his fist on the table, shouting that we were not receptive or appreciative of his constructive criticism. He finished his tirade with, "By the way, we're moving!"

Two weeks later, the movers packed our belongings, including the portrait. The furniture, once wrapped in thick brown packing paper, was stacked in tight corners of the living room. My brother and I found secret tunnels, intricate alleys beneath our belongings. We played hide and seek in the maze for three days, unsure where the hidden routes would lead us. The truck finally came to take everything to a container ship. Again we were moving, this time back to the States. My parents offered to bring Marta and Luis with us, to help them find work, to start a new life. But they wouldn't leave their families. They offered to keep Casique, and we gratefully accepted. My father told me we were moving to the small state of Connecticut, which I needed to learn to spell correctly. I could already spell Philadelphia, San Juan and Mexico, which were the other places I had left behind. Unsure of my native tongue, I spoke two languages, slipping effortlessly, often unknowingly between them. "We're going home," my mother said, meaning the States. I'd never been to Connecticut and couldn't think of it as home. My father added, "Your *mother* will like Connecticut. It's *safe* there." I wondered if anywhere would ever feel safe.

As I gazed at our family portrait, my eyes finally rested on my father. Although the style of the painting was slightly impressionistic and somewhat blurred, for the first time, I saw my father clearly, a man who searched for redemption in the wrong places, hurting the ones who could love him most. He sought redemption for sins of the past, but his guilt followed him from country to country, from battleground to battleground, unable to escape it. I set the painting on the floor of my living room, leaning against the wall. It stayed there for several weeks as family and friends came and went, commenting, "What an unusual setting, at the dinner table," or "Why don't you hang it up?" When my brother came for dinner one night, he too stood in front of it for a while. I asked him if he wanted it for his home. "Not really," he said. "It doesn't evoke the best of memories." I suppose all families have memories that are best left covered up. A few days later, I wrapped it up and placed it back in the storage closet for safekeeping.

Nine
Angola
(2004)

After lunch, I thank the trustee inmates before Gary and I return to the van.

The day has turned dreary. The clouds are blending into solid grey, with long tendrils extending down like jellyfish. The rain is coming.

"We'll see if we can beat the rain, but I have umbrellas in the back just in case," Gary reassures me. We turn back onto the gravel road, which eases up onto a levee that runs along the Mississippi River. To my right I look down at the swift current, flowing even faster than we are driving. My mind flashes to playing childhood games and building natural forts with my brother and cousins along this same river behind my grandparents' home. We were always respectful and cautious of the current, as Papa Luke would threaten us if we stepped even one foot into it. Here at Angola, it provides a natural barrier for prisoners trying to escape, as nearly all have drowned who attempted it. To my left, everywhere I look, I see land – 18,000 acres of it, mostly farmland. This fertile river soil is the same earth my grandfather used to till on his farm. My brother, cousins and I helped pick his watermelons, cantaloupes, tomatoes, eggplants and zucchini, popping figs and kumquats into our mouths as we worked and played under the hot summer sun.

From a distance, the inmates look like farmers. "What do you grow here?" I ask Gary. He lists cabbage, corn, okra, onions, peppers, soybeans, squash, tomatoes and more. "We produce four million pounds of vegetables and crops a year to offset the cost of feeding inmates here and in other Louisiana prisons. Inmates are paid 10 cents per hour to work the fields," he says almost boasting. *A modern day variation of a slave planation,* I think. *From before the Civil war to now, there have always been prisoners here.*

In the distance, I see low-lying buildings scattered miles apart from one another. It's a wide-open campus, not the typical cellblock kind of prison I imagined. After a while we descend to a simple grey building with a large "F" spray-painted in black on it.

"What's this?" I ask, both of us remaining in the van.

"We have several housing areas at Angola: Main Prison, which houses most inmates, and Camps C, D, F, J and Death Row. The camps operate as smaller prisons within the main prison, each maintaining different degrees of security. The most dangerous inmates live in individual cells, or lock down units, but for the most part, the prison is set up dormitory style. It breeds a stronger sense of community among the men." From what he tells me, though, the pastoral setting of sparse-looking villages dotting the landscape is misleading. Even with all the wide-open spaces, prisoners are tightly controlled. No one goes anywhere without permission and no one ever disappears. There seems to be a mind numbing routine for those who call the prison home, where every movement and item must be accounted for, where meals are served at the exact same time every day, where head counts are performed throughout the day, where showers only last three minutes and where "lights out" never varies. There are so many rules that no man can be expected to remember them all.

"This one, camp F, houses trustee offenders."

"What does that mean, exactly?" I ask, although I gather it is the safest.

"Over time, these prison inmates have earned a certain amount of freedom, like the men who just served us lunch. They are allowed to leave their individual camps, with close supervision of course. Some are waiters, farm crew leaders, ministers, all different jobs."

I consider the irony of *prison, freedom* and *camp*. I suppose over time, in a place like this, everything becomes relative. I wonder which camp Nathan lived in, or perhaps he lived in several over the twenty years he was here.

"What do you know about Nathan Wolfe's time here?" I ask, attempting to maintain my journalist composure and paint my own portrait of Nathan. After so many years of making him invisible, now that he is gone, it seems strange that I am trying to make him reappear.

"I did some research before you came. He started in H, maximum security, and made it here to F. I never met him and don't know very much about him, except for the fact that he had some trouble adjusting when he first got here. Most inmates do."

Gary tells me that ninety percent of the inmates who enter the gates of Angola will die in Angola because they're the worst of the worst, and in Louisiana, life means life – and ultimately death. The average sentence is 90 years. Very few will ever walk out of here.

"They don't accept it at first. They fight back. After about ten years, they settle down. Some even try to make something of themselves, like Nathan. He rose to a trustee level before he died … you know, for good behavior," he says.

There's that term again, I think. My temples begin to ache. I dig in my purse to find two Tylenol and pop them in my mouth.

"Would you like to see the last dormitory he lived in?" Gary asks me, still parked.

"Will there be inmates inside?" I ask tentatively.

"Not during the day, unless someone is sick," he says. "They're working in the fields or other jobs. We keep them busy and tire them out from dawn until dusk."

I doubt I'd be allowed into any of the more secure camps with violent inmates anyway.

We walk inside. There must be over 200 beds. I scan the room quickly and see only one inmate in bed asleep at the far end. It has an industrial feeling, with bare metal frames, thin mattresses and all white sheets. Nothing extra. "All they get is a bed and a trunk for possessions," Gary tells me. I wonder which bed was Nathan Wolfe's. I wonder what kinds of things he had in his trunk. Did he have pictures of his family? Books? Keepsakes? My breathing becomes shallow and tight. I cannot believe that I am in the same room where he slept and lived, where I am now breathing the same air as him. I feel my lunch turn to acid in my throat all of the sudden. Gary looks at me intently and says, "Ready to move on?"

"Yes," I say. *I've been trying to for a long time*, I think. We make our way back out to the van.

Ten
Alea-Jacta-Est

A red wood barn with white trim sat on the edge of our property in Wilton, Connecticut. It could have been a charming postcard of a quaint New England landscape surrounded by a still backdrop of the rolling hills covered in golden yellow and umber leaves. A winding gravel path led from our house to the red barn, which had two stalls, one inhabited by a tired quarter horse named Danny, who we adopted from elderly neighbors no longer able to care for him. The other sat empty in anticipation of my father's prized Argentinean thoroughbred to be transported from Uruguay once we moved back and settled from the expatriate life.

In his eagerness, my father had the barn built and purchased Danny as a sidekick for his awaited thoroughbred. He'd paid more than he was willing to admit for this dapple gray, wild-eyed stallion. As if he were a beloved child, my father refused to leave him behind. High-strung as a Triple Crown winner, his name was *Alea Jacta Est*, an uncommon and lofty name. Literally translated as *The Die Has Been Cast*, these were the words spoken by Julius Caesar after crossing the Rubicon with his Roman army, ready to fight the Turks and knowing they had reached the point of no return. We called him *Alea* for short. Standing seventeen hands in height, he was a beautiful animal. To my father, however, he was much more than that. He was a noble prince, a mighty creature with a majestic nature, a symbolic vestige of my father's Latin roots, and the world he was unhappily leaving behind.

A few months after settling in Wilton, my father made arrangements to have *Alea* flown from Montevideo to New York via Pan American Airlines. The process of safely transporting such a large and fragile animal from one continent to another was complicated. Unlike owners of Olympian horses or wealthy international equestrians, my father had limited knowledge and resources to orchestrate such a feat. He thought he'd made all the necessary arrangements with the airline and a veterinarian, whom he hired to properly sedate and travel with the nervous nine-hundred-pound horse on the eight-hour flight.

When the phone rang early Saturday morning on the day *Alea* was to arrive, my father expected it to be the confirmation that everything had gone according to plan, that he was boarded and en route to the Big Apple. Only a few hours remained before my father would drive to La Guardia to meet the flight, where he'd make sure his pride and joy safely disembarked and was brought to the mandatory international quarantine location where he'd stay for a few weeks before arriving at our quaint red barn.

But the veterinarian, still at the airport in Montevideo, called for a different reason. As my father stood speaking on the kitchen speakerphone, he paced and then sat down in a nearby chair. In Spanish, he said, "What do you mean? What kind of problem?"

I heard through the receiver, "Well, Señor Marbán ... I ... I don't know how to tell you. It was the engines of the plane. The pilot, he would not ... He ... expired on the runway. It was immediate. No suffering." Leaning against the table, my father's head now dropped into his hands.

"What are you saying? He's dead?" My father's voice was angry at first, then cracking like a child about to cry.

"Yes, it pains me to tell you, Señor Marbán. I believe he suffered a heart attack. The engines started with him on the runway. He couldn't take the noise, the shock."

"On the runway? Why? He should have been on the plane when the engines started. Explain this to me," demanded my father.

"He refused to board, Señor. The pilot grew impatient waiting. They keep a schedule."

"Why wouldn't he board? I want some answers!" My father pressed on.

But there were no answers. From all the information that was offered, or all that could be deduced, Alea had spooked, refusing to board on foot, into the padded, sound- proof stall that awaited him in the belly of the cargo plane, where he would be contained for the duration of the flight. The veterinarian sedated Alea to calm him down, hoping to get him to board. The sedation worked, but not in the way he had hoped. Alea lay down on the tarmac, right there below the plane. No one could rouse him. The pilot grew impatient because he had a schedule to keep. He started the engines. Alea's heart had burst, killing him on the spot.

I had never seen my father cry before, not even after the death of "El Viejo." He loved Alea as much as anyone could love an animal (or even a person). As if he'd lost a part of himself, he grieved for weeks. Yet his grief quickly turned to ire, which turned to us and then propelled him into months of litigation, suing Pan Am for negligence.

To the extent that my father had felt more at ease on Latin soil, my mother seemed to flourish when we returned to the United States. It wasn't just that she finally had command of the language or even the culture; her comfort seemed to lie in the small-town niceties of New England, the feeling of community and camaraderie among like-minded women and friends in whom she could confide. As if she'd simply subsisted in South America, she blossomed in this new garden where she'd been transplanted.

She became involved at our school, volunteered at church and began working part-time as a writer for *The Business and Commercial Reporter of Fairfield County*. As soon as Stephen and I were out the door for school in the morning, she threw on a nice outfit and headed into town to interview business owners who were opening, closing or making any significant changes – a woman on the beat, meeting people, doing research, making calls and fulfilling deadlines. It gave her a sense of independence and purpose that she'd lacked overseas, and perhaps she saw the writing on the wall. Within a year, she learned enough to strike out on her own, starting her own publication called *Market Place*, a similar publication, with different geographic boundaries. It was her first entrepreneurial venture. Month after month, she'd show us her latest edition, her words in print, concrete evidence of her own identity and ability. She was a bona fide businesswoman.

Most afternoons, I'd return from school to find her deep in concentration at the dining room table, intently hammering away on the IBM Selectric. Yet at first sight of me, she'd stop to join me in the kitchen for a snack. I'd rattle on about friends, gossip or schoolwork as she listened, genuinely interested. She could immerse herself in any aspect of my day, as if it had happened to her.

I thought we were happy in Connecticut. My father liked his new position with IBM and the comforts it provided. He continued to travel. Stephen and I settled into American schools with relative ease. With him in middle school and me in fifth grade, our world travels seemed to give us a leg up in many respects, especially in geography and Spanish class. Experienced in moving to new towns, we made friends quickly. My mother also found interesting friends: Helen, a talented landscape painter, Laura, a Portuguese beautician with her own salon and Deanne, a friend from church. They drew her out of her shell, encouraged her, for once, to pursue her own interests, primarily her writing, which seemed to anchor her and fill a void. They were her supporters, her fan club, her surrogate sisters.

My father didn't outwardly object to my mother's emerging passion, nor did he support it. He simply tolerated it. I don't remember ever hearing him acknowledge it, in fact, I wondered if he was even aware of it. He had passions of his own, which mostly removed him from the nucleus of family life. If he wasn't at the office or traveling, he was making wood furniture in the basement, developing photographs in his darkroom, or most often, horseback riding. His gusto for living, although impressive and even admirable, was self-focused and obsessive. With him at center stage, we simply sat in the audience, witnessing his perpetual fulfillments.

Early one Saturday morning, my mother, brother and I sat patiently on the bleachers at the Fairfield Hunt Club. We had risen before dawn in order to arrive early for an annual equestrian show, which drew riders like my father and fans from all over New

England. There was standing room only. During all of his spare time, my father had practiced in the ring behind our house, and this event had been the focus of his attention, and therefore the family conversations, for weeks.

It was a full day event, which we were agreeable, and also expected, to attend. My mother had packed snacks, brought the camera and a wide brim hat for the relentless sun. We watched rider after rider, until finally my father entered the ring sitting upright and regally on Don Tranquilo, Alea's replacement. He began the course at the far end of the ring. As he made his way through the jumps, the audience hushed so that all we heard was the horse panting, the hooves against the dirt, the echo of silence in the arena. At the jump closest to us, I could see the intense concentration on his face, where nothing outside of the ring or this moment existed. It was just he and his horse. With each jump we held our breath and when he took the last one, we stood, as always, to cheer for him. After the ceremony, where ribbons were awarded (he had a wall full of them), we met him at the barn to congratulate him.

The weekend following my father's horse show, there was an annual Chamber of Commerce award's ceremony to honor small businesswomen owners. My mother was thrilled to have been selected as a recipient for her business, *Market Place.* In her excitement she was up again at dawn. She had never received such an award. She readied herself all morning, brushed her curls and pinned them up into an elegant and professional bun, carefully selected her most business like clothes, applied just the right amount of makeup, and practiced her short speech over and over again in front of the mirror and me. I must have heard it five times.

My brother was in the living room, ready to go, but my father was nowhere to be found. We called out to the barn for him, looked around the house and everywhere we could think of, but eventually we had to go. Secretly upset that he was not there, my mother fell quiet on the drive. My brother and I, disappointed by my father's lapse, tried to cheer her up and talk about other things. The conversation wore thin. At the ceremony Stephen and I stood and applauded when she received her award and a gold necklace pendant in the shape of a book with the words "Market Place" engraved on it. Stephen and I were certainly proud of her and did the best we could to cheer her on, but we were hardly equipped to acknowledge her in the way she deserved. Later that night my father half apologized for missing the ceremony by explaining he was delayed with a horse farrier. Don Tranquilo needed new shoes after all the training for the horse show. "It's fine," said my mother with eyes cast downward and withdrawing in silence.

"What are you so upset about?" he snapped. "The kids were there and you got a necklace and award. How much more do you need?"

When it came to our successes, Stephen's and mine, my mother, alone, attended the recitals, school functions and awards ceremonies. She was our biggest cheerleader, exuding enough pride and enthusiasm for two. As for my mother's gains, well, I suppose we all fell short, but most of all, my father failed her, by sheer virtue of his age and his supposed role as her partner. Only years after my mother was killed, when I married and had my own children, did I fully realize the cornerstone she was in everyone else's success.

Our home back then was the epicenter of teenage activity. There were friends coming and going, parties and weekend barbeques, which all felt like happiness. My father was mostly away on business, but all of Stephen's and my friends loved my mother. They called her Mrs. Marbs. Sometimes our friends would stop by, even if we weren't home, just to hang out with her. She made them food and took time to be a confidante, a non-judgmental sounding board, always maintaining an open door for us or any one of our friends.

As for my parents' social life, entertaining was the one thing they still did well together. Perhaps with more people around, they didn't have to face each other alone, as taut silences had now become their common language. My mother prepared interesting and delicious food, while my father mixed drinks and told jokes, which everyone laughed at while Frank Sinatra sang "Fly Me to the Moon" on the record player. The act of entertaining served as a diversion from what was really going on — the gradual splitting apart of a glacier from deep inside, an ever-worsening break, invisible from the top, but ultimately doomed to crack. A house divided, my father lived at one end and my mother, brother and I lived at the other. Increasingly, there was an underlying anger in my father's humor, revealing more about himself than the victims of his jokes. What started out funny, frequently turned biting and hurtful, sometimes resulting in tears of family members and even friends. It had clearly been mounting since we returned from South America, where he'd felt dominion over everything and everyone, especially my mother. But the die had been cast. In my father's mind, he'd become a stranger in his own fortress.

Eleven
Half Heart, Half Blood

Three teenagers exited the jet way into the gate area of La Guardia Airport, where my parents, brother and I waited anxiously. I was nine years old, standing close to my mother, waiting to welcome my two half-sisters and half-brother. In my hand I held two roses for my half-sisters, a gesture my mother had orchestrated.

The night before, my parents sat Stephen and me down in our living room and carefully explained that my father had three children from a previous marriage who were coming to visit us for the first time. While I had a vague notion that he had been married before, I felt something between excitement, like a magician had just pulled a rabbit out of a hat, and confusion. *Why had my parents never fully explained all of this before, and what other secrets could they be keeping from us?* Since meeting Abuelo on his deathbed, I was becoming increasingly more aware of the complexity of my family and my parents' sins of omission.

After my father introduced everyone, we five children, ranging in ages from nine to fifteen, stood awkwardly in front of each other, trying to absorb our striking resemblances: thick dark hair, angled jaw bones and deep set almond shaped eyes.

Back at our home in Connecticut, following an hour and a half car ride of forced small talk and silence, my three new half siblings – Carlos, age 15, Annie, 14, and Susie, 13 – sat on the sofa together, while, Stephen, 11, and I sat with my mother on a nearby love seat. My father sat in a tall armchair amidst all of us, clumsily trying to drum up conversation, while fidgeting with my slinky on the coffee table. Shy and silent, we children were all data-collecting, developing profiles and trying to understand this new terrain.

"Tell me, Annie, do you like to play the piano?" my mother asked, knowing that their mother was a pianist and teacher.

"It's okay. I don't like to practice, though. It's boring." Annie twisted her long braid draping over her shoulder.

"That sounds familiar. Stephanie plays the guitar and hates to practice as well."

My mother leaned back so we kids could see each other. Our eyes met and then darted toward the carpet. Despite my mother's best intentions, our relationship could not be forced. We had to find our own way because we were old enough to know what was real and what was not.

"Stephen can beat a fine rhythm on the drums," my father said.

"I can beat a fine rhythm on Susie's back," Carlos chimed in. We all laughed, grateful for some comic relief.

Taking Carlos' lead, my father picked up a pair of maracas from the coffee table. "Check out *this* rhythm." He began dancing in the middle of the room, tripping over himself, acting like a drunk doing the Cha Cha. Everyone howled. There he was, center stage and under the limelight he always enjoyed, making everyone laugh and temporarily diffusing the underlying discomfort we all felt.

Later that evening, as my mother kissed Stephen and me good night in my bedroom, she said, "It may feel strange at first, but they're part of our family. You'll see. It'll get easier with time."

More than strangeness, I felt tenderness toward my half-siblings, because I knew they were growing up without a father. But I wondered about my father -- about his complete absence in three of his children's lives and his difficulty in making things right. He'd abruptly dispelled my belief that all parents give their children an equal measure of love. I wondered for the first time if he could abandon me in the same way. His lighthearted humor now seemed like a form of denial or a small Band-Aid for a deep wound.

Carlos, Annie and Susie occupied Stephen's bedroom across the hall. After lights were turned off and doors pulled shut, we all lay awake next to our full bloods, silent at first, letting the darkness finally relax our minds and release the tension of the day.

"They seem nice," I whispered to Stephen.

"Yeah, it's weird, though. They look like us."

"Yeah, Annie looks like me and Susie looks like you. Carlos is a blend, don't you think?" I asked.

"Maybe. He seems kind of funny."

"Funny ha-ha or funny weird?"

"Funny ha-ha. Did you notice he laughs a lot like Dad?" Stephen said.

"Sort of. Why do you think Dad never sees them?"

"No clue."

The weight of the question hung heavily between us.

I imagined that Susie, Annie and Carlos must have been speaking similar words among themselves across the hall. My parents, finally alone in the den, were speaking in muted tones, assessing the day's progress, until the sound of my mother's crying and father's angry voice broke through.

"It's the least we can do. You haven't paid alimony in years and she feeds them on food stamps," my mother pleaded.

"Why should I pay her anything? She's poisoned them against me."

"The children are innocent in all of this. You and I are the ones who must atone," she said, her voice cracking.

What were my parents guilty of? My stomach tightened, as it always did when they fought. I lay awake long after I could hear Stephen's breathing become regular with sleep. At nine, I did not understand my parent's marriage. I only understood that they fought often, that there were secrets from the past, and that my mother seemed more invested than my father in my half siblings.

This first visit lasted a week. By the end of it, the five of us had blended together and found enough common ground to look forward to seeing each other again. Over the following summers and holidays, they came for longer visits, where we fell into some semblance of a rhythm. Stephen and Carlos shared a passion for horseback riding and worked together for hours every day at the stable in front of our house. Carlos' sense of humor was infectious and Stephen was drawn to him as the older brother he never had. Annie, Susie and I played games, worked in the garden and baked together. They were tender with me in my youthful awkwardness. The disparity between their lives and mine must have been striking to them, but if they felt any jealousy toward me, I never perceived it.

Little mention was made of their mother and I was secretly curious about her. *Who was she? Why had she and my father divorced?* The only mention ever made of her was when my father angrily cursed her. Strangely, my mother always seemed to defend her. One day I asked my mother about her. She paused to gather her thoughts.

"Well, she is Cuban, like your father. She is a very accomplished pianist. They met when they were young and your father says she loves her music first and foremost."

"Is that why they divorced?"

"Your father wanted a homemaker who placed him first in life," she said, gazing downward.

So Susie, Annie and Carlos were growing up with a mother who focused on music and a father who was angry and absent.

Within a year, Carlos came to live with us. My mother had encouraged my father to do this because of the difficulties Carlos was having at home in Georgia, where his mother now lived. Perhaps the influence of a father might help the general disorientation he seemed to be experiencing in his life. At sixteen, during the mid-sixties and Woodstock era, he was drinking, smoking, experimenting with drugs, taking risks and hanging around a tough crowd. His Cuban mother, a full time pianist and teacher trying to support her family, couldn't handle it. My mother, more so than my father, thought a change of scenery would be good for him and also an opportunity for us to know him better. She never hesitated to reach out to his other children, inviting them for holidays, summer vacations, whenever they could come.

But Carlos' stay with us was short-lived, just a couple of years. It didn't take long for my father to find too many faults with his first-born son, probably much like his own father had found with him. His hair was too long, he wasn't a strong student, he hung around the wrong people. When Carlos pierced his ear, my father asked him to leave, bearing no responsibility emotionally or financially.

"Did you mail the child support this month?" my mother would ask.

"Of course," he'd snap.

Later, she'd discover his lie and mail the check herself. When he'd discover her honesty, he'd retreat into silence, knowing he was wrong, that she was right. My mother's clear position on these matters and her newfound strength to stand up to him raised the stakes considerably.

My father's reticence toward his own flesh and blood registered clearly. He held back, unconvinced that he should draw them into our lives. I felt the balance of his favor tipped unevenly toward Stephen and me, which created ambivalent feelings: gratitude, yet guilt, because I wanted him to offer them a more equal measure of his love. He had five children, not two. Were Annie, Susie and Carlos paying the debt of their father's bitterness toward their mother? Was he trying to deny their existence because they were tangible evidence of his failure as the man he was supposed to be? Perhaps he was trapped in his own father's web, doomed, despite his own painful memories, to make the same mistakes of disowning his children. Perhaps the similarities were too striking, like an unwelcome reflection in a room full of mirrors.

Twelve
Mantra

My mother felt a lump on the side of her head above her right ear. Doctors' visits and tests resulted in a one-week hospital stay at Sloan-Kettering in New York City, an hour from our home. No one fully explained to me what was happening, that she had a tumor and that Sloan-Kettering was a renowned cancer hospital. I deduced the gravity of the situation on my own, by eavesdropping and feeling the vibrations of stress all around me.

"It's only for a few days, sweetie. You needn't worry," she said firmly, not convincing herself or me. After our eyes locked and a short pause, she softened. "Every time I start to worry about something, I say to myself, *everything will be all right*. There's no use worrying about something that hasn't even happened. Right? Chances are it won't ever happen. Why don't you give it a try?"

But of course I did worry, especially when I realized that the likelihood of surviving a brain tumor was as good as that of surviving a collision with a train. I was filled with dread.

My father went to work every day as if nothing out of the ordinary was happening, completely unconcerned. I went to school, sick with worry, chanting my mantra, *everything will be all right*, hoping to alleviate my all-consuming anxiety. I could barely concentrate on my work and picked at my nails until they bled. Coming home to an empty house felt ominous, as if it were a preview of what it would be like when she died. After a few days of rattling around the house alone, with no information about her condition and wondering how she was doing all alone in some hospital bed in New York City, I decided to find out what was really going on, to be by her side.

New York was a frightening place to a fourteen-year-old suburban girl. I'd never been there on my own, only on buses during field trips or in the back seat of the car with my parents. After school on Friday afternoon, without telling anyone, I emptied my allowance money from my piggy bank, walked to our small-town train station and bought a ticket. I boarded the train like a young warrior, with a combination of apprehension and determination and found a seat next to an attractive woman reading a magazine, who was about the same age as my mother. Perhaps relying on some false sense of security, I felt the comfort of her presence next to me, even though she never looked up from what she was reading. Feeling the hard rhythm of the tracks beneath me, the landscape changed as skyscrapers came into view and we pulled into Grand Central Station. Holding myself tightly, I carried my backpack through the rush-hour crowd, dodging one person and another, until I finally found the information booth, where I asked an attendant which subway I should take to get to Sloan-Kettering. Through a microphone set in the middle of a bullet-proof window, a disinterested lady said, "Green-line to Fifty-Third. Then, walk two blocks east."

I descended into the bowels of New York City. The dinginess and thick smell of urine made me feel as though I were stepping into hell. My heart pounded while I sat sandwiched between strange people, all older than me, with barely enough room to breathe, much less move. Acutely aware of my environment, I felt alarmed by so many people from different races, all speaking different languages, including Spanish, which was only a small relief to understand. When the lights went out between stations and the train stopped, I silently but furiously chanted my mantra, fully aware for the first time of the meaning of claustrophobia. Just when I thought I'd explode with fear, the lights came on and the doors opened at my station.

As the temperature plummeted below freezing, the massive building came into view just before dusk. I walked through the large lobby doors across the worn marbled floors to the information desk of Sloan-Kettering Memorial Hospital. "The room number of Jeanne Marbán, please," I asked feeling rather small. The woman behind the desk gave me the room number, which half surprised me. I couldn't believe that I'd made it all the way to this point without getting stopped, mugged or lost. But there I was, finally, just steps away from seeing my mother. When I walked into her room, I felt myself shivering, unsure if it was from the cold, my nerves or the sight of her lying in a hospital bed with a bandage wrapped around her head like a mummy. Her surprise in seeing me was only equaled by my relief that I had made it. Her wide hazel eyes seemed larger than life as her look of surprise gave way to a look of concern, which gave way to a warm embracing smile. I fell into her arms, tears streaming down my face, unable to speak. She immediately assured me that everything was fine, that the tumor turned out to be benign and that she'd be coming home in a few days. "What's benign?" I finally asked. "It means that it's not cancer. It's just a bump. I'm going to be fine, really! See, everything turned out alright."

Yes, she would survive this. She had been lucky again, just as she had been lucky when the bullet missed her head in Uruguay. But I was keeping count and I knew about "three strikes you're out." As if I was the one with cancer, my secret dread of losing her was growing inside me, wondering not if, but when, it would finally happen.

It wasn't my father who retrieved me from the hospital that night, but my mother's friend, Deanne, the decorator. Late that evening, she drove into the city to take me home, but not until I received repeated reassurances from my mother that she'd be home in a day or two. Exhausted and deep in thought, we drove home in silence. Despite the wonderful news, I felt a penetrating longing for unspoken things to be set right, wishing my father had been the one to come.

A few months after my mother returned home from the hospital, a call came while I was sitting with her one night in the living room. It was anonymous, my mother told me much later. A man's voice. Brief and to the point.

"Is this Mrs. Marbán?" the man must have asked.

"Yes it is," said my mother casually, thinking perhaps it was a sales call.

I watched my mother's face darken as the man began to speak. I knew it was devastating news. After he spoke, there was a very long pause, a deafening silence.

"Who is this?" she demanded.

In that split second, suspended in place and time, she sat motionless, her entire world suddenly reduced to this exact point and nothing else. With a small, reflexive impulse, an involuntary spasm of adrenaline, she asked, "Who is she? How do I know you're telling me the truth?" But she knew.

Her hand now limp, the phone parted from her ear as I heard him say, "She works with him . . . no reason to lie to you . . . telling you because you're a good person . . . deserve to be treated better than this. Do what you wish . . . I thought you should know. Good luck, Mrs. Marbán." I heard him hang up. She could barely place the phone on the receiver.

Perhaps a malignant tumor would have been an easier prognosis than finding out her marriage was over. It was a different kind of death, one where she'd have to go on breathing. And I suspect it would have been easier for my father, at least that's what a piece of paper I found buried in my father's desk seemed to indicate.

I entered his office one afternoon, searching for a pad of paper to do my homework. I sat at his desk carefully rummaging through the papers. Trying not to mess up his piles of expense reports, bills and work documents, I finally found a yellow legal pad with his writing on it. There were two columns: "reasons to stay in the marriage" and "reasons to leave." Under the heading to stay were two things, "children" and "brain tumor." Under the heading to leave were a whole list of criticisms, too many to remember, an angry missive. I took the pad to do my homework, but could barely think about my assignment, as his list kept repeating in my head. I ripped the sheet from the pad and buried it in my room, never mentioning it to my mother.

So it was true. My father was having an affair and wanted out. All of my friends' parents were still married. I didn't know what divorce looked like. I didn't want to know. I just wanted to be in high school having fun. All of this occurred sometime between homecoming dance and Christmas of my sophomore year in high school, when I was on fire, in love with my first real boyfriend, oblivious to anything outside my own sphere. My parents' rocky marriage loomed large, but it was also in the backdrop. I was trying to move on. My social life reigned above all else, blinding me to my mother slowly sinking into new depths of depression.

She hired a detective who, over the next few months, followed my father everywhere. On one of his business trips he checked into a hotel under the names of Mr. and Mrs. Marbán. The detective took pictures of him brazenly leaving the hotel holding another woman's hand. It must have been brutal for her to see these –the irrefutable and ugly truth.

Late one night, my mother presented her findings behind closed doors. I heard the rise in their voices from my bed. I got up holding onto my pillow and moved down the darkened hallway toward their room to hear what was going on. It seemed that eavesdropping was the only form of communication I could rely upon. It was the worst I'd ever heard them fight – her pleading with him to end it for the sake of the family, him telling her that he didn't love her anymore. Her crying. Him yelling. At first I crouched onto the floor outside sobbing into my pillow. The walls were closing in on me, until I couldn't stand it anymore. Too many years of confined emotions about my parents' turbulent marriage finally propelled me like a missile into their room, yelling louder than both of them, crying, "Stop it! Stop it! I can't stand another minute of this. Mom, you're a doormat for letting him walk all over you. Just end it. End it now. Both of you." And that's exactly what they did.

The vibrant flame I had seen in my mother over the past few years was extinguished in one breath. With each passing week and month, the tears didn't stop. She looked disheveled and broken, barely able to take a bath or make it to the grocery store and back. My father moved out. Stephen was away at college, already a freshman at Tulane University in New Orleans, not far from my mother's family. He'd fallen in love with this city and chosen a university there, after all of our summer vacations. I was the only one left at home with her and knew she was in trouble. On Friday nights, when I went out with my boyfriend, I'd leave her sitting in the living room, either crying or staring into space, fearing what I might come home to in a few hours. I think now, she must have felt similar to how she did in the aftermath of the fire on her graduation night, only I didn't know what to do.

"You know as well as I do, honey, that your mom needs us now," Aunt Joy finally said to me over the phone. "She needs to be with you, Stephen and us. We are her lifeline. Stephen's already here, so you and your mama need to move to New Orleans. Do you think you can do that for her?" Selfishly, I didn't want to offer it up, and if only I'd known that New Orleans, where she'd encounter Nathan Wolfe, were anything but her life line, perhaps I would have rebelled more.

Two weeks later, after the car was packed, my mother waited at the end of the driveway for me to say good-bye to my father. He stood waiting for me by the barn. Despite all of his deceit in previous months, his eyes now filled with tears. He could barely speak. After I walked away, just before pulling out of the drive to head south, I turned to see my father standing alone in Alea's empty stall. It seemed my mantra no longer worked. I never understood why they called New Orleans The Big Easy, because in the middle of high school, it felt like the most difficult thing I'd ever done.

Thirteen
Angola
(2004)

One hundred and forty miles northwest of the Big Easy, Gary and I now leave the prison dormitory of the man who took my mother from me twenty-four years ago. I'm not sure if it was another lifetime ago or yesterday. So many years and events have blended together, I can't be sure. Neither am I entirely sure of why I am here and what I am seeking.

We come to what seems like a small town within the prison. Gary explains that this is the guard/employee village, which houses about 200 employees who live and work here with their families. Kids are bused in and out of the prison to outside schools. The rest of the 1,200 prison staff come in and out every day from nearby towns that basically exist to support the prison. "Angola is the main employer for a hundred miles," he tells me. I can't imagine living in a prison compound to do my job, but I recall how desolate my drive to Angola was. And like my mother, who eventually had no alternative but to work in a convenience store, many people must do whatever jobs they can in order to survive. It's a means to an end.

Farther on, I see that this village sits in the shadow of Warden Cain's mansion at the top of the hill. *This prison is Cain's life*, I think. "Both the employee village and the mansion were built by inmates," Gary adds. "The inmates do it all here."

As we continue to drive, Gary points out the dog kennels, where Bloodhounds, German Shepherds, Dobermans, Rottweilers, and wolves are bred and trained to attack unruly or escaping inmates or sniff out drugs or contraband. One looks exactly like Casique, our guard dog in Montevideo. I imagine they trained these dogs in a similar fashion, with sticks wrapped in fabric and dipped in meat. "We are proud of our dog operation here," he says. In my research, I

81

previously read that they breed shepherds with wolves to make more vicious attack dogs, almost like Josef Mengele. Dogs that would make Casique look docile.

The gravel road takes us past armed prison guards on black and white Percheron horses. These powerful workhorses, originally from France, are a colorful vestige of Louisiana's French colonial ancestry. Standing even taller than Alea Jacta Est, guards ride alongside inmates walking single file toward the fields for a hard day's work. I hear Sam Cooke's famous "Chain Gang" playing in my head. The majority of the inmates here are African American, but there are white men, like Nathan Wolfe, as well. They dress in plain clothes, jeans and T-shirts, like any other men. Not the typical prison uniform.

"Angola loves its horses too," Gary adds, as we pass a large stable. There is an inmate out front giving a horse a bath. Both seem to be enjoying the cool hose water while the inmate glides a sweat scraper along the horse's belly. "We have quarter horses, Percherons, thoroughbreds and mules. We cross breed them and use them for different purposes, even sell some at auction or to other law enforcement agencies." *More mad breeding experiments,* I think.

In many ways, though, this place does not feel like a typical prison I'd imagined, and I am surprised by the workings and sense of community that has been created. It's an isolated working prison farm, where everyone has a job.

"What kind of work did Nathan do?" I ask. As if I am deconstructing a riddle, I am gathering clues to create Nathan in my mind's eye.

Gary is not sure. "Most men do different jobs over the years. Everything from farming and machine repairs to construction, cooking, cleaning, or basically anything and everything it takes to maintain their existence. They all have a hand in it." After pausing, he redirects our conversation, "You're a journalist, right?"

"Yes," I say, trying to remember anything outside of this place.

"Then maybe you'll appreciate this." He hands me a magazine called *The Angolite.* "It's published six times a year by our inmates, and it's won many prestigious national awards. We believe it's good for our inmates to publish an independent magazine. Gives them a sense of purpose and recognition. Check out the latest issue." He points to a headline. "Angola Inmates from Incarceration to Assimilation."

Clever, I think. A catchy title and personal interviews on how inmates adjust to prison life. "May I keep this?" I ask. It reminds me of my mother's newsletter, *Market Place.* She would have been interested in this, I muse.

"I brought it for you. We have many subscribers on the outside too," he adds as he hands it to me. I actually consider it.

Fourteen
Down in the River to Pray

Like a harmonic convergence, my mother's clan, the Cutreras, had always gathered for Sunday dinners at my grandparents' home in Braithwaite. The four sisters, Jessie, Frannie, Joy and now my mother, back home after twenty years, and their families were all expected at the table each week for a loud and raucous Italian dinner, usually spaghetti and meatballs. Pots clanging, the screen door slamming shut after children running in and out, my grandmother hollering at my grandfather to do this or that, all felt like familiar chaos. There were up to twenty of us crowded around the elongated, vinyl-covered kitchen table, sitting on chairs, boxes, stools or whatever else we could find. Seldom could a single voice be heard above the rest, except when the food was served. As if someone had hit the mute button, everyone savored the first few bites. Then, one of the sisters would finally say, "Deee-licious mama, as usual. Mmm . . . mmm." Slowly, by the end of the meal, the deafening pitch would rise again.

I once loved the visits to my grandparents' two-bedroom, single-story country clapboard house, resting only a few hundred yards from the Mississippi River. Built after the fire, the house sat up on stilts and was only slightly more luxurious than a double-wide trailer. During my earlier childhood summer visits from Montevideo with my mother and brother (my father stayed back to work), I fell silently and contentedly in line at the kitchen counter between my grandmother and mother, rolling meatballs and stirring spaghetti sauce, listening as my grandmother gossiped about everything we missed since our last visit. "Mama, what ever happened to Lucy and Sam?" my mother would ask about some neighbors up the road.

"Oh, Sam, that good for nothing scoundrel. He ran off with some office girl and left Lucy to raise them children by herself. But he got what was coming, blindsided by a truck and lost his leg, his car, his job, his new girl, everything. He came crawling back to Lucy. Can you believe the nerve of that man?"

"So what happened?" she asked. I listened with sonar sensitivity.

85

"That crazy woman forgave him and took him back. But, I'll tell you, she makes him pay for it every day. That man doesn't get a moment's peace. She makes him do the cooking, cleaning, laundry, anything she can think of to lighten her load. Maybe she wasn't so crazy after all!"

"Sounds more like vengeance than forgiveness!" my mother offered.

I heard a lot at that kitchen counter, never sure what to make of it all, but I relied on the natural order of things, my place among three generations of women, standing side by side, making meatballs and spaghetti sauce. After all the meat was rolled and the sauce simmered, we played poker with pennies at the kitchen table, where my grandmother, a fierce little Italian woman, would pull out her jar of coins, giving my brother and me ten pennies each to start. Within a few short games, she'd win our money and everyone else's back.

During lazy afternoons, I took long walks along the Mississippi River with my grandfather, Papa Luke. A gentle giant at six feet four, he had the biggest hands I'd ever seen. Like a dried-out riverbed, they were covered with dark hard cracks from working on his farm. He held my small soft hand while we walked on top of the levee, telling me how he'd helped the Army Corps of Engineers build it years before, helping to protect his farm from flooding during hurricanes when the Mississippi overflowed. This same levee extended for two hundred miles, all the way to Angola State Penitentiary, where the inmates worked to secure the levee as well. It seemed as if my mother's essence would always come back to this river, even in death.

Here with my grandfather, standing fifteen feet above the river, we had a clear view of my grandparents' serene little farm on one side and the raging river waters on the other. Eventually we'd make our way to his orchard, where I ate figs and kumquats off his trees. On the bench swing, which hung from the giant willow, he'd tell me stories from his childhood in Sicily and why he believed in God. Despite his being illiterate, he was the wisest, kindest man I ever knew. Yet, my grandmother would get mad and yell at him all the time because he could hardly hear. "Lukey, hurry up and go to the market for some bread. Madonna! That man can't hear!" Or maybe he just pretended not to.

My mother seemed happy during my childhood visits from South America. The muscles in her face relaxed, there was a glimmer in her eyes, she threw her head back and laughed from her belly. Late at night I'd hear the four sisters talking and laughing out on the patio, reminiscing about old times. Jessie, Frannie, Nettie and Joy. They were a seemingly inseparable foursome, who spoke their own private language. During our summer visits, aunts, uncles, cousins and high school friends came to this small place where my mother was raised. They came to see us, but mostly my mother. The minute we were around them, her southern accent returned. She called everyone "y'all" and "sugar." I had loved seeing her like this. But when my father arrived at the end of the vacation to bring us home, all of the sudden she seemed busy and tired again. She was changed by his unspoken judgments and expectations.

Now, twenty years later and divorced, the idle chatter of adults and the frenetic antics of my rambunctious cousins served, on some level, as a shock absorber for my mother's crushing grief. Yet on another level, it was déjà vu or perhaps her second of three deaths. The fire had taken her down once, and now, she was again amidst the smoldering ashes. Although her family had always been her anchor, New Orleans was not a place she thought she ever wanted to return to permanently. Unemployed and single after twenty-two years, my mother found herself back in a life and place she had outgrown, a life that held an almost forgotten dark secret. Like a solid body under water, she moved among her once-again-worried family in slow motion, in a trance-like state. There were no clues about what to do next, how to survive the paralysis of divorce, how to go on breathing. She was deluged, awash at sea.

For me, New Orleans had always been somewhere we spent magical summer vacations while living overseas, but not a place to live. I was now halfway through my high school years and forced to attend an all-girl Catholic High School, among girls who had grown up together. Their friendships were already set, and they were totally disinterested in a Yankee girl with a bad attitude. I understood my mother's predicament, but I had been robbed of vital things too. I had left behind good friends, a large home in the countryside of Connecticut and my first real love, Chris, a kind, intelligent boy with whom I was just discovering my sensual self. Now I had no friends and was in a small apartment in a congested unattractive city suburb. My head and heart were at war.

Early one Sunday, in the heat of summer, a few of us gathered before our traditional dinner. "Let's take a ride up the river," my mother suggested. "It would be good for the children to experience this." At least she hadn't lost her interest in family field trips and was recalling something positive from her past. Seven of us, my mother, brother and I, along with my Grandmother, Aunt Joy and her children, crammed into my grandparent's Oldsmobile Cutlass to take a twenty-minute ride up the river, where the Mississippi makes a sharp bend between English Turn and Pointe la Hache. There, the Mississippi waters slowed enough that, on a good day, a person could stand waist deep without being swept away by the current. On other parts of the river, we often saw entire trees and heavy debris floating by.

Pointe la Hache was black Baptist country, home to the poorest of the poor. We parked by a small, whitewashed, one-story building, just on the other side of the levee and walked toward the river. When we arrived, my grandmother greeted Pastor Isaac, Beatriz's widowed husband. Beatriz had passed after a long bout with cancer. Annie had cared for her toward the end, just as Beatriz had tended to Annie and the Cutreras for so many years. Pastor Isaac was a tall man in a long white robe. Clutching his Bible, he said, "Y'all mos' welcome ta join us." He raised his arm to the rest of us, who stood inside my grandmother's shadow.

The river was the color of coffee, a shade or two lighter than the skin of the twenty or so church members from Ebenezer Baptist Church, who gathered at the water's edge. In Sunday dress and floral hats, the women raised their hands up to their Redeemer, eyes closed and swaying, as their soulful voices sang an old gospel tune a cappella and in two-part harmony.

As I went down in the river to pray
Studying about that good ol' way
And who shall wear the starry crown?
Good Lord show me the way!

We stood up on the levee, maintaining an expected distance from the others. We were silent witnesses, voyeurs, of a sacred act. My mother had also witnessed this in her youth, probably in this exact place, and wanted to share it with us.

Like her, I had been raised a good Catholic girl, with hymns, prayers and rituals etched like cave drawings on the inside of my skull. My first Holy Communion, with white dress, gloves, patent leather shoes and a lace veil on my head, was an ethereal event. Taking that holy wafer into my mouth for the first time, as the body of Christ dissolved on my tongue and the incense wafted into my nose, eyes and lungs, I was infused with goodness and lightness, as if I were a floating white feather, as if every cell in my body had been cleansed. Cleansed of sins I hadn't even committed. And then there was the wine, the forbidden fruit, of which I was allowed a small sip every week, consciously swishing and savoring the taste after the chalice touched my lips. Even through high school I had gone to confession regularly, spilling out my infractions through the thin screen between me and God's henchman. "Last week I told my brother's girlfriend he had diarrhea the first time he asked her out," or "I lied to my parents about taking a bath every day." I went on religious retreats, attended mass weekly and played my guitar while singing and swaying to Kumbaya with the church folk group.

I participated in these rituals of cleansing, renewal, atonement and forgiveness perhaps out of my parents' sense of tradition. I did not necessarily question their significance or anticipate that I might later summon prayers my mother taught and recited with me each evening on bended knee at my bedside. From before the time I could speak, my mother had taught me to talk to a higher power in my own words and through such prayers as The Lord's Prayer. If I remembered nothing else, it was the entreaty to *forgive us our trespasses, as we forgive those who trespass against us.* As if it were a law of the universe, a karmic truth, the required balance of our forgiving others in order to be forgiven ourselves, seemed to comfort and guide her. I would not know how deeply she instilled this holy mantra in me until encountering Nathan Wolfe.

The church members approached the muddy embankment, where the Mississippi lapped up onto the shore. They tightened their circle around a young man, not much older than I was. Fully clothed, Isaac walked into the water, holding the boy's hand and pulling him along until they were waist deep in the murky water. The boy looked frightened, in full knowledge that this river had claimed too many lives, from the overpowering current or the deadly water moccasins that slithered just below the surface.

Pastor Isaac tightly embraced the boy with one hand on his shoulder and the other on his head, lowering him into the water until he was completely submerged. Then he raised him up, hollering, "Do you see da light, my son?" The boy, stunned, shook his head no. And down he went again into the cold water. The church members sang even louder.

> *O sisters let's go down*
> *Let's go down, come on down*
> *O sisters let's go down*
> *Down in the river to pray*

The next time Pastor Isaac raised the boy from the water and asked him if he had seen the light, he vehemently shook his head yes and hollered, "I seen da light." My brother and I stood transfixed by the event, while my cousin Kimmy whispered, "If that was me, I would've made sure I seen it the first time!" The boy's fear turned to a strange ecstasy, probably the dizzying effect of a lack of oxygen, adrenaline and hypothermia . . . or maybe the Holy Spirit. Pastor Isaac and the boy trudged out of the river, where they were handed bath towels. The boy's parents embraced him. A slow procession started over the levee, people ambling back toward the little white-washed church. We followed along behind, still at a distance, listening to the hymn in softer tones now. I noticed my mother fell back from the group, walking toward the water's edge by herself as everyone moved in the opposite direction. I stopped, silently watching what she was doing, half-worried and half-knowing that she was completing her own rite of passage. She took something small from her pocket, heaving it high and hard toward the river. As it flew through the air, I saw a golden glint reflecting against the sunlight, just before being swallowed and carried away by the river current. She wrapped her arms around herself, stood for a moment with head down and turned to walk back toward us. I met her half way, asking her with my eyes, yet already knowing what she'd done. Her wedding ring. I walked beside her quietly, back to the church, where we sat in the very last pew. The final verse rang out in full volume as if the walls would burst from it.

As I went down in the river to pray
Studying about that good ol' way
And who shall wear the starry crown?
Good Lord show me the way!

Pastor Isaac delivered a short and feverish sermon with flailing arms and an inciting tone, bringing his flock to an emotional pitch. I had never experienced such a charismatic and theatrical service. Standing on the sidelines, watching their unshakable faith and impassioned spirits, I wanted something like it for my mother, something to sustain her, especially since I would soon be leaving her, or she leaving me. Now more than ever she, and soon I, needed to be shown the way.

Fifteen
One More Time

The music pulsed through my veins while the lyrics challenged my brain. I lay alone in the middle of my dorm room floor with a pillow propped under my elbows. The stereo played at full volume while I read the words to Pink Floyd's, *The Wall*. Stephen, a true music aficionado, had mailed me the newly released album. It had arrived the day before, but I had waited for the right moment to savor it, along with half a joint that my bohemian flower child friend, Maggie, from down the hall, had given me earlier. A new chapter in my life had begun and I was fully absorbed in it, feeling for the first time the simplicity of only worrying about myself and shedding the weight of past family events. In the fall of my freshman year, as the cool crisp air was sliding into winter, I was ablaze with anticipation, like the emerging deep umbers and reds just outside my window.

Leaving New Orleans had been a relief, but leaving my mother was complicated. I was worried about her. My only consolation was that she still had my brother, who attended Tulane University and lived only fifteen minutes away. In the end, my father's very aggressive divorce attorney was far more ruthless than my mother's and she was left financially stripped of the life to which she had grown accustomed. She was forced to close her small business when we left Connecticut. After a failed attempt in her late forties to go back to school and become a nurse, she was now working as a cashier in my Uncle Paul's package liquor store on Chef Menteur Highway, on the depressed outskirts of New Orleans. It was so seedy that he gave her a small pistol to carry in her purse to protect herself, a pistol that was only a foot away from her when she was killed, a pistol she was untrained, or perhaps hesitant, to use. But the job provided a few extra bucks in her pocket and some promise of security, as my uncle was soon planning to retire and sell the store to my mother at an affordable price.

Bitterness from the divorce ravaged both of my parents, while I lived on eggshells, always worrying and wondering how I could ease things, especially for my mother, who had lost her will to fight. Like a porcelain china doll tossed to the ground, her spirit had finally been shattered. She was a shadow of her former self, and I often wondered if I'd come home to find her dead by her own volition. In random moments, my mind could easily conjure her in bed after an overdose of pills, or even worse after having used the gun my Uncle Paul had given her to work in his convenience store. *What would I do? Who would I call?* I'd been worrying about her death all my life, it seemed.

We both knew I had to go, though. It had been her dream that, unlike her, I would go to college. "A woman, even more than a man, needs an education," she preached repeatedly. After all of her expatriate experiences and traveling half way around the world as the wife of an international business executive, she was ultimately a non-degreed divorced housewife. "You never know what cards life will deal and you should be financially independent," she lectured.

I'd applied early decision and was accepted for a pre-med track at Emory University in Atlanta, eight and a half hours by car from my mother. My father wanted me at UConn, the more inexpensive state school near him. But I knew I couldn't be that far from my mother. I'd written him a letter appealing to his intellectual logic, outlining all the reasons I needed to be at Emory: my love of science and desire to go into medicine, the school's fine reputation and the fact that it was a geographic compromise between him and my mother.

In the last few months of high school, the relationship between my mother and me took a turn for the worse. In addition to being worried about leaving her, I was angry for being displaced in my last stretch of high school and felt secretly burdened as her emotional caretaker. I started dating a cook at a local French restaurant where I worked. He was a good looking but ambitionless Cajun boy with a reckless drinking and drug habit. Perhaps out of boredom, or just defiance, I began drinking, smoking, coming home late and disregarding my mother. One night, on my way out for the evening, she and I were arguing about what time I had to be home when a joint fell out of my pocket and bounced off of her foot. We both looked down. Without a word, I stooped down, picked it up, put it back in my pocket and left. Later that night, when my drunk and stoned boyfriend's car skidded off the highway landing on its side in a ditch, I had to call her to pick me up. She drove me home in pouring rain with her hands trembling on the wheel, tears streaming down her face. I was too proud or angry to apologize. Perhaps I thought it would be easier to leave for college mad than sad. And perhaps I was selfish enough to want what every teenager wants – independence. If only I'd had a crystal ball, I could have assuaged my relentless remorse later on.

Going away to school – away from negative social influences – eventually seemed the best solution from all angles. So, over that summer she helped me buy my colorful comforter, desk lamp, alarm clock and toaster oven. She had a hand in all my comforts for my new home away from home. Finally, the day came when she and I flew to Atlanta. She helped me unpack, made my bed, attended the orientation and talked me through my nerves, just as she always had. Later, standing on the curb as she pulled away in a taxi, all the turbulence of the past few months dissolved. She pressed her hand to the back window as I waved good-bye, with the tears rolling down both of our cheeks.

~~~

A loud knock on my door, perfectly timed with the trailing words, "All in all you're just another brick in the wall," brought me back to earth. It was Jerry, a senior I had been casually dating for a few weeks. He was bright and ambitious, a business major, and interested in a more serious relationship than I was. I kept seeing him because he was fun to be around and uncomplicated. And he had a car. "Lunch?" he offered. I'd lost all track of time and realized I was, in fact, quite hungry.

Lingering over another less-than-edible meal in the cafeteria, he said, "I've got four tickets to the Joe Jackson concert at the Fox this weekend. Wanna go?" he asked. It was fun to get off campus occasionally, and I was ready for a change of pace.

The concert was that Saturday, January 15, 1980, a cold night, the temperature dipping below freezing. He picked me up in his ten-year-old silver-colored Datsun 280ZX, which he'd named "Hi Ho Silver." I kidded him about being the Lone Ranger and me being Tonto. Jerry's roommate and his date joined us. We headed downtown to Peachtree Street for a cheap dinner at Felini's Pizza before heading to the Fox Theatre, an exquisite concert hall fashioned after an Egyptian and Moorish mosque.

The concert scene was rowdy. In the bathroom before it began, I stood next to a girl with a red-spiked Mohawk, stiletto-heel boots and more body piercings than I'd ever seen. Her friend helped her unfasten her black leather body suit. This was another world, beyond our preppy college campus.

Later, when the band started playing, the floor vibrated from everyone dancing. Song after song, the music became contagious and before long I was dancing too, feeling uninhibited after a couple of beers and a joint. When Joe Jackson's, *One More Time*, thundered through me to a crescendo, I was oblivious to anything other than the music and myself, dancing as the strobe lights whirled in multicolor flashes and the loud music blasted from the speakers.

When the concert ended, Jerry drove us all back to campus. We were all quiet in the car, perhaps numb and exhausted from the loud music and highly charged night. He wanted me to spend the night, but I declined. He was irritated, I could tell, as it was our fifth date and he had certainly been courting me. Although I felt guilty about it, I just wasn't attracted to Jerry in that way.

"Why not?" he asked.

"I can't, Jerry. I don't feel the way you do . . . not yet anyway," I said as kindly as I could.

"Maybe you'll feel differently if you just give it a chance."

"I just can't, but thank you," I said firmly, kissing him and stepping out of the car.

A relationship with Jerry, let alone anyone, right now felt too complicated. I wanted to remain unencumbered, light and loose. I had found an oasis at Emory and nothing was going to infringe on this.

Sixteen
Angola
(2004)

About half way through the tour I need to use the restroom, so Gary drives me to the visitor's center, where friends and family visit inmates. I enter a lobby area where a large woman stands behind a caged desk with a clipboard, checking people in and out. He walks me in and tells me that I'm allowed to enter with greater ease because Nathan is gone. Even still, before I arrived I had to supply them with a list of what I'd be bringing with me. "Prison policy," he says. "We closely monitor who comes in and out and what they bring with them."

The fluorescent lighting overhead fills the windowless room, antiseptic and devoid of character and warmth. Two corrections officers escort an inmate past me, each with a hand locked on his forearm. He is handcuffed behind his back. *He must be one from maximum security*, I decide. In a split second, his eyes connect with mine and then drop to examine my body. I look downward, uncomfortably, wondering if, perhaps, I'm wearing the wrong outfit. Black slacks and a green blouse. I worry that it's too revealing, even though I've given it considerable thought before arriving.

I try not to look at anyone directly, but can't help steal an occasional glance, wondering now about the other visitors. There is the large, middle-aged woman in a dress with two fidgety toddlers sitting next to her. Could she be the mother of an inmate, bringing her grandchildren to see her son, their father? Across from them is a strikingly thin girl. Her stamina appears to be an unnatural wonder, as if she has fasted herself thin. Angel wing tattoos stretch across her ashen white bony shoulders. She takes long drags on her cigarette. A girlfriend or sister maybe.

I wonder how many times during Nathan's twenty years here had he received visitors. Had they ever come through this room to visit him? I ask Gary. He doesn't have a record, he tells me. I am unsure if he means not one visitor in twenty years or that he simply doesn't know, but I assume the first.

97

He goes on to say that Angola tries to promote visitations, even host an Annual Family Rodeo to bring families together. But Angola is a long way from anywhere and it's too hard and expensive for many friends and family members to make the trip after a while. They eventually stop coming.

It's as if they are no longer people here, removed from society, taken off the grid, as it should be. Victims like me would just as soon lock them up and throw away the key. Over the years my hatred and anger toward Nathan and people like him have bubbled up like acid, ready to explode inside of me. But still, I cannot believe no one came to see him in twenty years.

I glance at the men, women and children who have come to visit inmates. *Who are they? What are their stories? What peace have they made with the wreckage these inmates have created in their lives?* But their faces reveal nothing. They are all weathered stone. I once believed that murder happened to other people, in other families, in other places. But here I am, in a prison where my mother's killer was sent and I am a visitor, just like these people. Like me, the families of the prisoners are also forgotten victims of the crimes. They have lost a loved one, and additionally, are forced to share guilt that is not theirs, questioning what they might have done differently to avert the horrible crimes their relatives have committed. Society assigns blame to them as well, and they become the targets of reproach.

I wonder, just as I did of Leonora and Francesca, our servants in Mexico, *Why am I different from them and how have I been born into my life and not theirs?* I suddenly feel a strange connection to these visitors, as if we are all the same, only I am visiting a dead man, because I was too afraid to visit him when he was alive. I wonder if this experience, this tour, this investigation, whatever it is I am doing here, will give me closure or just make me even crazier. From where I am standing right now, I have no way of telling.

Seventeen
Camera Obscura
(1980)

My memory of the murder could only be seen through an artificial eye, a camera obscura, where images were conjured by lighted reflections in a dark box, undefined as illusory or real and therefore questionable. Everything around that time yielded something like a series of candid photographs lined on a wall, all leading up to and following something significant, yet each one bore no knowledge of the other and I, as if standing alone in the middle of a darkroom, was as clueless as the photographs themselves.

At first I was thrilled when my brother, Stephen, and Aunt Joy, who lived in New Orleans, appeared in the hallway of my dormitory. They emerged from the stairwell as I was on my way to the restroom. Stopping at first sight of them, my mind could not register their out-of-context presence from 800 miles away. When my mind, making an unrealistic leap, caught up, I thought, *what a great surprise*! But in a flash, their stricken faces registered. Now on unsteady ground, I asked, "What is it?" Aunt Joy gently took my elbow and guided me into my dorm room. Stephen and then my roommate followed, closing the door behind us. I searched their faces from one to the other. The weight in their eyes and the tightness in their jaws made my chest constrict.

"There's been an accident," said Aunt Joy.

"Who?" I asked, thinking it must be my grandmother.

"Mom," said Stephen, barely audible.

"Is she alright?" I felt the air leaving the room.

Like a sledgehammer descending upon me, Aunt Joy, barely able to speak the words, said, "No, honey. She's been shot. She's gone."

The following seconds and moments played out in still frames, one picture collapsing into the next. A loud sound came from deep inside me, a low-pitched wail, a sound I didn't even know I could make. My knees no longer reliable, the weight of my body unbearable, I fell to the ground and doubled over, with my head on the floor. My aunt and brother huddled next to me, all of us kneeling. There were no more words, just shoulders shuddering and uncontrollable sobs, undistinguishable by whom or for how long. I could no longer feel my limbs.

A small crowd gathered in the hall, outside my door. Word must have spread through the dorm. My roommate, slipped out to speak with them. No one knew what to say, all of them stunned mutes, feeling pity, all secretly thinking, *I'm sorry this happened to you, but I'm glad it wasn't me.* As the shutter divided each frame, we threw random things in a suitcase, went from my dorm to the taxi to the ticket counter to the plane. Two hours later, thirty-thousand feet in the air, traveling five hundred miles an hour toward a place I would no longer call home, I sat quietly between my messengers, disoriented and numb. Staring at Aunt Joy's hand wrapped around mine, it was the same shape and size as my mother's, the one that used to draw the letters of the alphabet on my back so I would learn them as I drifted off to sleep at night. It was the hand that pulled me to her chest when I had nightmares. It was the hand that blew a hundred teary-eyed kisses and pressed against the car window just a few months ago when she left me at school for the first and last time. In an instant, my mother, and my life as I knew it, were gone forever, without even a good-bye.

How could I not have sensed that something had happened that night? It was as if the electricity had been turned off and I hadn't noticed. We'd always been connected to one another. The summer before I left for college, as we'd done many times before, she and I immersed ourselves in reading the same books, then compared notes and impressions; we lay in her bed on rainy evenings and weekends discussing the supernatural and eating cherry Twizzlers. We had both read *The Reincarnation of Peter Proud* and *Many Lives Many Masters*. Fascinated and convinced that there could be an afterlife where spirits communicated with loved ones, we promised each other that whoever died first would contact the other. I remembered this promise in the days that followed, desperate to maintain my

100

connection to her, to defy what had happened. But I heard and felt nothing, except a dull pounding ache in my head and chest.

Snapshots of a funeral reveal broken images and random oddities lodged in my mind for no apparent reason, such as the phone call to my father, with Aunt Joy, Stephen and I sitting on the edge of the bed in Aunt Jessie's bedroom. Aunt Joy dialed his number and handed me the phone. I hadn't spoken to him in months, as the divorce had ended badly and I'd been privy to too much information, souring any desire for contact. I told him she'd been shot at a convenience store where she worked, that the funeral was in two days, that he could attend or not. Aunt Joy spoke after me, asking for financial assistance with the funeral, for which he hesitated. And she, in a fit of rage, told him that he was not welcome at the funeral, that it was because of him that my mother had been forced to work in such a place, that it might as well have been him who pulled the trigger.

Then, there were the muted conversations at my Aunt Jessie's kitchen table discussing the arrangements for an open casket, traditional for an Italian funeral. "I don't want an open casket," I said, fearing that my final image of her in death might be too awful to live with. Better to remember her living, I thought. "Oh, honey, it's the way it's always been done in the family." I was silenced, unable to fight this battle. I followed the flow of things numbly, letting myself be swept along.

The day of the funeral I struggled with what to wear. I stood in front of my closet painstakingly unsure of how to dress correctly for such an incorrect event, even asking myself, *what would she want me to wear?* It was the first of a million questions I would ask myself for the rest of my life: *What would she say? What would she do? What would she want me to do?* Her death was a storm that left me like a rudderless boat with no compass. Eventually, out of sheer exhaustion, I settled on a black skirt and boots with a grey top. What difference did it make? I just needed to get through the night.

We rode in a big black car across town, through the French Quarter down to Louisa Street. When we arrived, we were escorted to the back room. My brother and I were led to the coffin of an unrecognizable woman wearing my mother's lavender and lace dress, pearl-drop earrings and amethyst ring. Her face, fixed in time and like a French Quarter harlot's, was entirely too made-up. I could see the stitching that someone had done to sew her matching lavender eyelids shut. Although her body was there, she was nowhere to be found. I was certain her soul had fled. My eyes wandered down to her left breast, where I knew the bullet had entered. What had they done about that, I wondered? Frozen in horror, I slowly inched my way backward, against a wall into which I tried to disappear.

At some point afterward, a distant uncle I'd never met approached Stephen and me, placing one hand on each of our shoulders. "I know you don't remember me. I'm your Uncle Frankie. I want you to know, if either of you ever need anything, anything at all . . . a difficult relationship, someone giving you a hard time, whatever the case may be. You call me. I'll take care of it. You understand?" A more homely image of Marlon Brando flashed through my mind as he handed us each a business card. We thanked him and put it in our pockets. After he left, Aunt Frannie told me the reason we never met him before was that he had just gotten out of prison for money laundering, working for the mob. I'd forgotten about meeting Uncle Frankie until decades later, when I found his card folded within the many sympathy cards and letters I saved, like mementos of some rite of passage.

Following the funeral, there was a short memorial service in a chapel adjoining the funeral home. Who spoke and what was said completely escapes me, but one image that surfaces in this line up of photographs in my dark room remains permanently imprinted in my mind and heart.

Stephen and I were sitting next to each other, shoulder to shoulder, sandwiched between my aunts. My father had chosen to adhere to Aunt Joy's request of not attending the service over coming to support Stephen and me. Sometime in the middle of the meaningless words and rituals, Stephen quietly and almost invisibly crossed in front of me and made his way to the sacristy, a darkened room on the side of the altar. My eyes followed him. Instinctively, a few seconds later, I followed him. When I got there, he was leaning with his hands and head against the wall quietly sobbing as his chest and shoulders heaved uncontrollably. It was the first time I ever remember seeing him cry, as crying was not allowed by my father, particularly not by men. I moved toward Stephen, wrapped my arms around him and embraced him tightly. We were one body in grief. In an unusual role shift for the two of us, as he had always been my protector, I tried to reassure him, "It'll be ok … we'll be ok." But I was not at all sure of this myself, nor do I think he was either. Although there appeared to be a sea of people and extended family around us, we clung to each other like shipwrecked survivors, each of us a life raft for the other. It seemed we had only each other now, as my father had created another life for himself. A few moments later, we pulled ourselves up, straightened our crumpled clothes, wiped our eyes and returned to the pew.

The days immediately following the funeral are lost. I was stranded in purgatory, a frozen place between here and there, where consciousness is suspended or eliminated, as if in a murky holding tank. Discussions, decisions and arrangements surrounding logistical matters of what to do with her house, her belongings, her physical life were going on all around me. Whether I was unable or simply spared, I was not a part of this, although I wish I had been. I had no idea then how much I'd later treasure any remnants of her life.

I emerged to return to school a week later, shocked to find a note with a five-dollar bill in my campus mailbox.

Hello Angel,

Here's a little something extra for some toothpaste or deodorant from your proud mother. I'm off to work now. Speak to you Sunday.

Love, Mom.

Half out of my mind, time stopped. I lost my already shaky bearings. *A message from beyond,* I thought. As blood drained from my face, the floor beneath me tilted. I found the nearest bench to sit down on. *Was she fulfilling the promise we'd made to contact each other?* Then I looked at the date. She had mailed it on her way to work that night, just hours before she was killed. It was so typical of her, sending a little extra cash whenever she could, a care package of cookies, a news clipping she thought would interest me, always maintaining a connection in between our weekly telephone calls on Sunday. As if suddenly war-wearied and overcome with fatigue, I had to return to my dorm room to sleep.

My exterior surroundings at school bore no trace of what had happened. Classes, friends, parties, everything the same. Unless I brought it up, it was as if the event had vanished into thin air, erased from the photograph, with no physical proof. But my interior landscape bore the evidence, for it was entirely different, stripped of all familiarity and knowledge of the terrain. I'd been blindfolded and dropped in a foreign land with no road map or ticket to get home. I knew I had to try to resume a "normal" life, but "normal" was a term I no longer understood. Like fumbling blindly inside the black box, I managed to attend classes most days, fitfully sleeping other ones entirely away. Often confused, I'd forget to study for an exam or go to my part-time job at a fancy restaurant, where I was a hostess. Some days I teetered on the edge of insanity, when hysterical laughter would turn to an uncontrollable crying jag or I'd wake up, thinking it had all been a nightmare. The usual college drinking made it worse. I had trouble knowing where my dreams ended and reality began. My dreams offered convoluted alternatives for what had really happened. In one of them, my mother called on the telephone to tell me she'd been in a mental institution and was finally coming home. In my dream, I sobbed with relief. I sobbed so hard that I woke myself up, unsure if I'd really received such a call. Just before I picked up the phone to call her number, to see if it had all been a terrible mistake, it all came crashing down on me and I suddenly felt like I weighed a thousand pounds again. Disoriented and exhausted, I wondered if a mental institution wasn't where I belonged. Like the reflection of the Camera Obscura, everything seemed an illusion.

In the beginning, Jerry called frequently, inviting me here or there, for dinner or a movie. I made up excuses: a biology test. Anything. Promising maybe next weekend. But when he'd call again,

I'd say I was going out with friends. Out with my roommate. Or I wasn't feeling well. Excuses. Always excuses. The pauses in our conversations grew longer and longer.

After so many constructed intricate excuses, eventually, he stopped calling. He wanted to take care of me, to help me figure it all out. I had nothing to offer him. I wanted to forget that I'd been with him that night, that anything about the evening existed. I was too tired to think, to care about myself, much less anyone else. I wanted to sleep, to lose myself in a place where no one else could go. My grades dropped. With a D in calculus, I was barely able to maintain the required grade-point average to stay in school. After a brief hospital stay for a severe intestinal illness, I made the decision to lighten my academic load, dropping calculus, removing myself from the pre-med track, which was the first tangible evidence that the life I thought I would lead would now be much different.

As a child, I had grown accustomed to moving from country to country, house to house, but I had never felt homeless. My mother's death knocked me off my axis, as if she had been my earth and I her moon, orbiting around her in space and time. Wherever she had been was where I called home and her absence set me loose in the universe, floating aimlessly, untethered and alone.

Somewhere in my peripheral vision, or maybe a blind spot in the mirror, there was a murder trial, an entire theatrical event with the New Orleans District Attorney, Harry Connick, Sr. (father of the famous pianist and crooner), a jury of ten, four witnesses, the media and of course an accused killer with his two accomplices, both of whom copped a plea bargain by turning him in. Behind the scenes, probably among my aunts, it had been decided that I should be spared the horror of meeting Nathan Wolfe face to face in a courtroom.

Eighteen
Bamboo Scaffolding

I dream I'm in a large canoe with friends, paddling up the Chattahoochee River. Fighting a steady current, our oars are in rhythm, cutting through a cool emerald wake, inching forward against resistance. We perspire, straining to row beneath the brilliant sun, splashing each other, teasing, and conversing as college friends do. The nearby shoreline slopes deeply, coated in thick green kudzu, strangling the other vegetation.

Suddenly I notice a smaller canoe coming downstream toward us, but off to the right. In it is a woman wearing a tan trench coat with her collar turned up and hands in her pockets. No effort is required on her part as the stream carries her along. She is wearing dark sunglasses with a scarf over her head. The only visible part of her body is her ashen face, staring straight ahead, with no expression whatsoever. In an instant she passes by. I am aware that the woman in the trench coat is my deceased mother. I am perplexed, feeling a flash of profound sadness.

I continue on with my friends until we find a large pool of still water where we abandon the canoe to swim deep beneath the surface among colorful corals and fish. Further down, I see a small shipwreck. I realize that I can breathe underwater. My body glides freely, unencumbered by weight, my skin cool and porous.

My roommate for the remainder of college was Marian, a bright girl from Tennessee, a reluctant pre-med student and a talented musician and singer. We first met as freshmen, in the stairwell of our dorm one night, a few months after I returned from the funeral. She was sitting by herself, playing her twelve-string guitar, singing Joni Mitchell's "Big Yellow Taxi," which echoed in the hollow stairwell like a hymn in the Cathedral of Notre Dame. In that moment, she became my sanctuary. With her closed eyes, she was lost in her music. Her expansive vocal range and perfect pitch lured me to sit on a nearby step. There was nothing but the music. I couldn't remember ever hearing anything so pure and beautiful. After she finished, she opened her eyes to find me sitting there. I introduced myself, but she already knew who I was. My mother's murder had given me some unwanted notoriety in my dorm. I learned that her mother had been a Nashville singer who taught her two daughters how to hold a microphone before they could hold a bottle. We talked for hours. After she found out that I spoke Spanish, she taught me the harmony of a simple song called *"Siempre (always)."* We sang into a hollow stairwell, where for a few brief moments I lost myself, my sorrow temporarily suspended, and heard my own pure voice for the first time since the murder.

That first summer after my mother died, between freshman and sophomore year, Marian came to live with me in New Orleans, carrying her guitar, looking for an adventure, distracting me from the strangeness of living in a place that no longer felt like home. We rented space with Stephen and his roommate on Liberty Street, an old part of town, in a dilapidated un-air-conditioned house from the early 1900s. The heat and humidity were oppressive, but we tried to focus on other things, like our air-conditioned jobs. I worked in a revolving rooftop restaurant downtown, where I could count on a good meal and a view of the city every night. Marian got a job singing in a nearby pub. When we weren't working, we mostly sat around Stephen's living room, drinking gin and tonics, smoking weed, talking, and listening to Marian play her music. On Sundays, occasionally, Aunt Joy invited us over for spaghetti and meatballs. We piled into Stephen's old Chevy Nova and drove out to her house in Chalmette, on the edge of the ninth ward that Katrina later swallowed whole. Aunt Joy made sure that when we drove off, we had enough leftovers for half of the next week. Having Marian with me that first summer kept me from slipping into the whirlpool I circled constantly, always threatening to engulf me.

It was Marian's first time to New Orleans. She wanted to see and do it all: Sunday mornings at the French Quarter flea market, late-night jazz bars on Bourbon Street, afternoons at the Audubon Zoo, riding street cars up and down St. Charles Avenue, all with me as her tour guide. Some afternoons, we'd buy 50-cent snow cones and sit on top of the levee, watching the Mississippi flow by. She helped me stay afloat that first summer, like a life preserver, always tuned in to when my mind began swirling, always turning the smallest things into adventures, forcing me to find the surface and sometimes even laughter.

That fall, we returned to Emory, with me seemingly still intact, at least on the outside. Although I was born a few years too late to call myself a flower child, I rode the coattails of that era in college, over a decade later, in the 70s. Somewhat reservedly, I trailed *The Grateful Dead* with friends on weekends, dancing unabashedly, twirling under the misty moonlight and under the influence of magic mushrooms and weed, looking for enlightenment and answers, while also trying to forget. One highly charged night, in the middle of *It Must Have Been the Roses*, the dike broke and tears spilled forth like a gushing river. I felt the full magnitude of her death, and then only moments later, as if I had finally expelled all of my sorrow, I began to laugh uncontrollably, until my stomach ached. Wondering at first if I had lost my mind, I finally thought I understood the truth, that joy and sorrow can co-exist equally. If only it could have been that simple. Perhaps Nathan Wolfe had thought he'd find some truth on drugs as well, or maybe he was too far gone, just miserably addicted and lost. While Jerry Garcia's guru status offered some semblance of an embrace that night, the cold and hollow anticlimax of the next day, and many more like it, left me dangerously at loose ends. I no longer believed, as once promised, that my nightly recitation of The Lord's Prayer could "deliver me from evil," or anything else for that matter. However, as if some invisible reins pulled me back, I retreated from the edge of what felt dangerously close to insanity. I vowed to quit the hallucinogens. Perhaps fear, or something larger than myself, was working in my favor.

The thought of therapy had come and gone, as my father convinced me that it was a hoax and that all therapists were crazy themselves. Nadirs and zeniths were interchangeable. When I couldn't pull myself back up, I called Stephen, who was back in New Orleans, trying to graduate Tulane and handle the debris and rubble from my mother's death.

I suppose I might have been labeled as complicated, confused, even intense. But there was also the lightness of typical new romances, parties, road trips, midnight dormitory antics, dinner with friends and other college fanfare. I tried not to miss out, and if I did, Marian and other friends wouldn't let me. The dark lows came frequently and intensely, but I began to let them wash over me, to let them inhabit me instead of fighting them, until they had their fill and released me until the next cycle.

The second summer after she died, Stephen and I backpacked in Europe. He had graduated and this was a gift we gave ourselves with the money from the meager settlement of my mother's estate. One afternoon we sat in a café in Athens, Greece, just outside of the Acropolis with the Parthenon as the backdrop, sipping Cokes and eating moussaka. We were parched and hungry after spending the morning touring the ancient temple of Athena, goddess of reason, intelligence, arts and literature. Our backpacks were snug between our feet, as the night before we'd slept in a youth hostel where a group of Germans had their backpacks stolen, passports and all. It was a real trip stopper and a costly misfortune. We were already operating on a tight budget nearing the end of our eight-week trip.

Stephen had spent every weekend of his last semester in college, painting and readying my mother's house for sale, while I was back at school in Atlanta. It was hard to be away from him, as he was the only one who understood the tenuous new world in which I was living. He'd also helped my aunts with the grim task of sorting through and emptying out the contents of my mother's home, much of which was stored in his small apartment. After the sale, we had enough money to buy two airline tickets, Eurail and Hostel passes for eight weeks of travel in Europe. "She'd want us to have this experience together," we told each other. She had always loved travel and learning, so we constructed a loose itinerary beginning in Holland and traveling through France, Spain, Italy, and finally ending in the Greek Isles. The truth was that after the crushing weight of the previous year, we both needed some escapism.

Before leaving on our trip, we'd bought identical red and black journals to record our impressions of the hundreds of sites we'd see together. At every café or youth Hostel, or whenever we were not in motion, we wrote in them. One of my first entries, just after we arrived in Amsterdam, reads,

"I can't honestly say I'm comfortable yet. I feel a combination of fear and excitement. Traveling with Steve is excellent, though, because we feel the same about so much."

After finishing every last bite of our moussaka, we lingered for a while, drained from the summer heat and weight of our backpacks. I'd started with eighteen pounds on my back, but it increased to thirty-six after so many open-air markets and other stops along the way.

I'd just finished an art history class and Steve, an avid reader and science nerd, had been like a tour guide for much of the trip. Our wonderment and conversation about art, politics, literature and history never let up. We had spoken little about my mother on the trip, as words did not suffice for what we both carried every step of the way. But here at this café, as we were coming to the end of our trip, we finally spoke of it.

"Do you think Mom is with us, that she knows we took this trip?" I asked.

He paused before answering. "I've thought a lot about it, Steph . . . while painting the house last semester, while moving all her stuff out of her place and into mine, and all along this trip. I've been trying to make sense of what the hell happened to Mom and why."

I listened.

"The way I see it, there are two choices: either it makes sense and there is some divine plan for what happened . . . or it doesn't, and this was just some random messed up event."

"Which one do you think it is?" I asked.

"I'm favoring the second."

This was the first time he'd ever spoken of his faith (or lack thereof) to me. He was a scientist at heart, always seeking to understand the way things worked. For as long as I could remember, he had his face in a book, exploring and pondering cultures, concepts, religions, philosophies, science and history. Once, in his early college years, he spent a few weeks checking out a commune on some island off the coast of Louisiana. He told my mother, who was still alive, that it was a religious community. She called it a cult, while she wrung her hands with worry. We were both relieved when he returned, seemingly satisfied and disinterested in joining. He was

111

well versed on mainstream religions as well more fringe ones like, Hinduism, Confucianism, Zoroastrianism, even witchcraft. His curiosity for knowledge of the world around him seemed limitless. In my youn`ger years, I had mostly tuned him out when he spouted facts and figures from his latest readings. Most of it was over my head and I did not have the insatiable appetite for learning that he did. But here in this café, in a foreign country, after all that had happened to us, and perhaps appropriately honoring the legacy of the great Athena, whose temple stood in front of us, I thought about the two choices.

"Sounds pretty existentialist," I said, proud of the fact that I even knew what the word meant. The waiter cleared our plates and refilled our water glasses.

"Exactly," he said. "Bad things happen to good people, right? Crap happens and there isn't necessarily any reason for it. Instead of asking why, I'm more interested in who I am because of it. I figure I'm the sum of all my experiences. Mom's death has loomed large and it's up to me how I interpret it."

I allowed his idea of no afterlife, no God, no meaning whatsoever, to wash over me. Despite our Catholic upbringing, which I'd previously and generally accepted with its wide margin of mysticism and the unknown, I had wondered about this myself after my mother's death. Atheism, however, was an extreme concept for me.

"I don't believe there is any meaning in the world beyond what meaning we give it," he continued. "I don't need to construct some delusional narrative for myself so that I can feel better about being alive, or assume that there is a God who ordained me for this experience with the intent of some great purpose."

I didn't feel like I'd constructed a narrative to explain my mother's death, or that I'd been ordained for anything through this experience, but I did feel anger that an almighty God would let this happen. "Sounds pretty chaotic and hopeless," I said.

"Not really," he countered almost optimistically. "Mom's death was a fork in the road for me. When bad things happen, people have to find a way to cope, right? Many people -- maybe most – choose a path that relies on faith. I'm not saying it's wrong, but it doesn't resonate with me. My path relies on *me*, which feels more logical and liberating than relying on an unknown being for some meaning I can't understand or accept."

"Are the two paths so separate?" I asked, almost pleadingly. "I mean, can't there be a divine being along with random crap?" Perhaps deep down I feared separation from my brother if our paths diverged, because in many ways it was in him that I now placed my faith.

"Not for me," he said, with all the gentleness and respect he'd always shown me. Yet I was not so sure.

That night we boarded a ferry for Santorini. Backpackers on a budget, like us, took to the upper deck for the night before arriving the next morning. Wealthier passengers inhabited the interior rooms with private bedrooms and baths and a common dining room. Tired from our long day in Athens, Stephen and I claimed a small corner of the deck, ate our dinners that we had carried on board from a portside deli, and stretched out next to each other in our sleeping bags. As the boat gently rocked to the soft waves of the Adriatic and the warm breeze blew clouds across a moonlit sky, we listened to other travelers speaking in Greek, Turkish, French, German, Spanish and Italian. Eventually, one of the travelers began to strum his guitar. The music and his words were foreign to me, but they carried me lightly over the dark ocean, embracing me in a way I had never been embraced before. As my body and mind drifted, suspended and unencumbered, I knew this moment with my brother would endure forever and was beyond anything I could write in my journal.

We traveled for another week before boarding our flight back to the U.S. where Stephen would start a new job, requiring him to move from place to place, and I would head back to try and finish college. We would be apart, but speak by phone or visit whenever we could. I finished my final entry in my journal at the airport, which read,

"This experience has been priceless, and I know I've changed in many ways. I'm so lucky to have had it. If mom was alive, she'd be beaming at the thought of our gaining so much."

~~~

After graduating college, I stayed in Atlanta, mostly because I didn't have anywhere else to go. New Orleans felt like the dark abyss. Stephen moved to Birmingham for a publishing job. Connecticut, where my father was living with Margaret, his third wife, felt uninviting and awkward. So I found a low-paying job working for an advertising agency. Marian and I rented a small apartment on Oxford Street, a cozy place on the second floor of an old brick building, which lay on the edge of the red light district in downtown Atlanta. Once we got past the junkies, prostitutes and homeless that convened on the street corner, we were content in our little abode. We had our own bedrooms and beds, which lay on a slant from the buckling floors and we shared a bathroom containing an old-fashioned claw-foot tub with a steady leak. It only felt like Chinese water torture at three o'clock in the morning, after the couple upstairs finished screaming obscenities at each other and having loud and pounding make-up sex. I wasn't even that upset about the cockroaches because they provided tangible evidence that I was eating enough to leave behind a few crumbs for them.

Within a year, I received a phone call one Sunday from my father. He'd been calling more frequently and I could tell immediately that something new was up. He told me he'd accepted another transfer with IBM, this time to Hong Kong. He and Margaret would be leaving in a month. I paused, unsure of how to respond. He sensed my unease and added, "We want you to come and visit and stay as long as you want. Can you think about it?" Strangely, I was sorry to see him go. My relationship to him had become like the orbit of a highly-charged electron around its nucleus. I circled in and out and all around him, never straying too far, drawn to him in ways I didn't understand. Perhaps out of need. More than ever before, he now seemed receptive, even selfless, perhaps out of pity. "Sure, Dad. Sure," I offered tentatively.

Not fully committed to my job and suffering from something between depression and wanderlust, I negotiated a leave of absence and sublet my room to a summer student so I could spend three months in the Far East living with my father and Margaret in their luxurious mountain top apartment overlooking Hong Kong Harbor. Maybe this is what I needed. Maybe traveling far away, as I had with

Stephen, would help me make more sense of the world, of my life. Or maybe it was just another distraction.

My bedroom window there was perfectly situated to observe the dichotomies of the city. From my sill, I looked down to the harbor to see lines of modern skyscrapers, many shrouded in bamboo scaffolding. Enormous yellowish tan meshes covered these massive bamboo skeletal structures, which were more solid than they appeared and an art form unto themselves, almost preparing for the unveiling of a new or renovated building. Due to typhoons, it was a city under constant construction. Similarly, the harbor itself welcomed enormous tankers or state-of-the-art private yachts drifting alongside small rickety wooden junks driven by old men wearing long robes, beards and Chinese rice hats, while rowing their wares to market with bamboo oars. Old versus new everywhere. Even half way down the mountain, in lovely modern neighborhoods and tree-lined parks, each morning I witnessed the ancient ritual of Tai Chi. Thousands of citizens poured into the streets or small plots of nature to slowly center themselves before starting their day.

The rhythm of Hong Kong began to swell within me. I felt the subtle shifting of old and the emerging construction of new, of fragile relationships with my father and Margaret becoming something more steadfast. They were all I had now. And they were reaching out to me. The grudge against them, Nathan Wolfe and what my life had become had been breaking my back and I needed to lighten my load, at least partially. Margaret often invited me on outings like taking the bus to explore the island or shopping in Stanley Market. I frequently took the ferry across to Kowloon side to meet my father for lunch. He proudly walked me around his office introducing me to colleagues. Over lunch we spoke more openly and comfortably than ever before. I felt his love more genuinely. I even found a part-time job through the *South China Morning Post* to tutor English to a Chinese national and earn a few extra dollars for my side trips into northern China and the Philippines. Everything was new and different. Everything was interesting. Yet everything was still the same.

Shortly after arriving in Hong Kong, I learned my father and Margaret were expecting a baby, another half-sibling of mine. This would be the first of two more half siblings, Heather and Holly. My father, now in his fifties, was starting his third family. I wondered if I would soon need a flow chart to explain the structure of my messy and confusing family. There seemed no end to my father's prolific, yet entangled life. Despite all of this, I was intrigued at the thought of being an older sister.

Halfway through my trip, Marian showed up, once again a welcome companion on whom I could always depend. On a shoestring budget, using student passes, Marian and I ventured off with our backpacks, making our way to remote islands in the Philippines and into southern mainland China, visiting famous sites. A highlight was visiting Po Lin, a Buddhist monastery on Lantau Island. I had always been curious about Buddhism, eager to learn more about the untethered concepts of suffering and materialism in the world. Like a heat-seeking missile being drawn to a nebulous target, I orchestrated our visit. We walked the gardens and meditated with cloistered, taciturn monks. Out of reverence, we didn't speak a word, except when we were alone, and even then, we whispered. The pure life of the eastern monks was a tall order for two western girls who liked gin and tonics, weed and loud music. It was even taller for Marian, a pack-a-day smoker. One afternoon, as I walked through the serene gardens, I caught a glimpse of Marian, sitting cross-legged underneath a low hanging Chinese Elm. At first I thought she was meditating, but then I noticed she was inhaling deeply on a menthol cigarette she had smuggled into the monastery. "What about the butt?" I asked her. She lifted a plastic bag conscientiously containing her butts from earlier in the day. "I'm not converting any time soon," she smiled.

Nineteen
Angola
(2004)

Gary turns up the radio as we make our way across to the other half of the prison farm nearing our last stop. Old gospel music fills the van. I am stunned that the song playing is "Down in the River We Pray." *Is this just a coincidence? What is happening here?* I wonder. My skin turns cold.

"This is our prison radio station," he says. "It's mostly Gospel and Christian programming. The inmates have coined it 'Incarceration Station.'"

The song ends and I hear the announcer say, "This is WKLSP, Incarceration Station, the best in the nation for sermon and sound."

"The inmates like rhyme and alliteration," I say, chuckling for the first time today.

As we pass a small chapel, Gary says that Billy Graham donated this one and that there are seven chapels at Angola, all built by inmates. I am curious about Burl Cain's concept of moral redemption, which I have read about and Gary mentioned over lunch. I ask Gary to explain it. He responds, somewhat by rote, "Cain believes that moral people are not criminals. That's why moral rehabilitation is the only true rehabilitation." He further explains that when inmates have a sense of purpose through work, education and faith, it usually results in inmates learning to live more peacefully and productively in a prison community."

I already know that human beings do not do well without hope, and prisons must be breeding grounds for despair. As if these men weren't already desperate and dangerous enough before they got here, I imagine that a despairing prisoner must be a dangerous prisoner.

117

"Sounds like Christian evangelism," I say, hoping I don't sound judgmental or skeptical, as I sometimes am about religious extremism.

"They are all interfaith chapels," he clarifies. "But Cain is a strong Christian and offers it up as a strong option. We do have a few Muslims, Jews and Mormons, though." Evidently, when Cain invited a Baptist seminary to open in Angola, he was surprised when they agreed, covering the costs with outside donations. "Inmates can get a degree in seminary if they want to become prison ministers. This has been a real game changer at Angola," he says almost proudly. Even a few Muslim, Jews and Mormons have completed the program, so that they can minister to their own people within the prison. "While not ideal," he readily admits, "many of the principles are the same." He goes on to say that moral rehabilitation has to occur in order for inmates to lift themselves beyond the jungle atmosphere that once existed here and still exists in many prisons, which endangers them and the staff. I wonder if or how much Nathan ever bought into any of this. "Cain's turned this place around since he got here in 1995. Violence and killings have been lowered by over 80% at Angola," he adds. As Gary rambles on about Cain's philosophy, I do the math. During his time at Angola, Nathan spent about 75% of it (thirteen years) before Cain arrived, when sexual slavery and rape, brutality, gang violence, rat infestation, no air conditioning and other inhumane conditions existed. And based on the little that I know of Nathan, he would have been a sexual slave, not a slave owner. Part of me feels he deserved every bit of it and more, and another part is secretly horrified.

Twenty
El Pescador

It took me seven years to understand the first commandment of grief: the more you avoid it, the more it plagues you. As a therapist would soon show me, the only way out of the room is through the room. Hong Kong had been an excellent distraction. I returned unenthusiastically to my advertising job in Atlanta. Sitting at my desk eating lunch one day, I saw an ad for a cheap weekend vacation deal to the Yucatán. I was still hungry for another adventure and was becoming a master of avoidance, staying busy no matter what. It seemed to be working so far. When I got home that night, I convinced Marian, now a medical student, she needed a break from studying, that we were both working too hard, that we deserved to spend a few days snorkeling, eating papaya and laying in the sun. My paycheck provided just enough money to cover the cost of my ticket and half of a cheap hotel. And her father was still supporting her, as long as she remained in medical school. We were two women in our mid-twenties in search of relaxation and adventure. We packed our bathing suits, sunglasses, sunscreen and a few sundresses. This was my first time back to Mexico since living there when I was six years old.

The first few days we swam in the ocean, drank margaritas poolside at our modest hotel, Las Brisas, watched the sunset, slept and read. It was a welcome respite from my job and her intensive studies. On our last morning in Cancún, we floated in a deserted cave pool, a short distance from our hotel. In the afternoon, we climbed the nearby rocks and found a spot to sun ourselves, like Galapagos seals. Marian, lost in a text book, and me in Gabriel Garcia Marquez's *One Hundred Years of Solitude*, spent hours without hearing the sound of our voices, just the lapping waves and call of seagulls. Later, we paddled back to our hotel, where we showered and at sunset, we walked to town for our last dinner. It had been a perfect day.

He was sitting with a friend at a table behind ours in a small authentic restaurant named *El Pescador*, The Fisherman. I had my back to them. Marian had already made eye contact when the waiter

119

brought us two tequila shots called "Cucarachas" from *Los Señores* from the table behind. Blushing, I turned around, slightly raising my glass to them in thanks, turned back and took a sip, gagging at the taste, while Marian chugged hers right down, then laughed at me.

"Conservative," she called me. "Reserved," I corrected. Admittedly, I was more reserved than she was, especially when it came to men. She was open, unafraid and much more willing to trust. I held back, always calculating the risks, which were forever in my field of vision. Her parents, in contrast to mine, were life-long partners – a foreign concept to me. After we paid the bill, she walked over to their table and introduced us. I hedged, standing a few feet back from the scene, observing the interplay.

He was undeniably handsome. Black hair, dark almond-shaped eyes, olive-colored skin, thin, with slightly chiseled features. *Latin?* I wondered, slightly off put by my father's cultural background and track record with women.

"I'm Michael," he said in perfect English, extending his hand professionally. He pulled the chair out for me to sit. Marian, already entrenched next to his friend, was having the time of her life. We went through the formalities of introductions and small talk. He asked where I was from and told me he lived in New York City. After speaking for a few minutes, he seemed more American than me. He'd come to Cancún to celebrate completion of his residency and convinced Howard, his friend and colleague, to join him. Then he leaned over and whispered, "He's going through a divorce."

Howard looked too young to be getting divorced. It was a good sign that he'd asked a male friend to join him and not a woman, unless they were secretly gay. But I didn't get that impression. No wedding ring either.

"Residency in what?" I asked.

"Oral Maxillofacial Surgery." My interest was piqued. Good looking *and* intelligent. *He's probably a jerk then,* my cynical mind flashed.

He asked about my job. We talked for a while, exchanging information about each other. A second-generation Syrian (not Latin), he was born and raised in New Jersey, from a large family with two parents who were still together, quite happily it seemed. His eyes, kind and deep, like the ocean pool we'd been swimming in earlier that day, drew me in. I floated in them, effortlessly, peacefully. Whatever I was saying made him smile. A wide and wonderful smile.

Walking on the beach later, we found a high sand dune. We leaned back and looked up at the constellations. "There's Andromeda," he pointed out. I strained to remember my mythology class. Andromeda was a beautiful princess who was chained by Poseidon, God of the Sea, to jagged rocks in the middle of the ocean for the sin of her parent and was rescued by Perseus, son of Zeus. A classic tale. I wondered if Michael had any knowledge of the story, if he thought of himself as my Perseus, or if he was just a smart scientist trying to impress me under the night sky. When the conversation finally paused, he said, "Tell me about your family." We were entering difficult territory now.

"Oh, let's see. My father lives in Hong Kong. My mother is deceased. And I have a brother in Birmingham." I hoped to leave it at that.

"Have you been to Hong Kong?" he asked.

"Last year. Marian came too. It was amazing." I rambled on about the monastery and our travels, bragging a little, perhaps. His interest was genuine and I didn't mind avoiding the topic of family. But eventually he came around to it again.

"How old were you when your mother died?"

"Eighteen."

"What did she die of, if you don't mind my asking?" There was no way out now.

I never answered this question smoothly, for fear of making people uneasy, including myself. It was often a conversation stopper, a dead end. Cancer or a car accident would've been an easier answer, more expected, I suppose.

"A freak situation, actually. She was shot in a store hold-up." There was the predictable silence.

But Michael didn't shy away. He continued, asking more questions, wondering how I'd coped. Finally he added, "I lost my brother-in-law and best friend the same way, two years ago." Now I was silent. I'd never known anyone who lost a loved one in a shooting, much less in a store hold-up. "It was my sister's husband. They had three children together." It was my turn to ask questions. The circumstances were remarkably similar to my mother's. My surprise morphed into a silent sense of connection, a bridge between two unknown worlds. After a while we came to the end of it, unable to say anything further about ineffable losses. We'd shared something deep for two people who'd just met, almost too revealing, like standing naked in front of a stranger, yet somehow comfortable.

The morning after I returned to Atlanta, sitting at my desk at work, the phone rang. The sound of his voice made my heart stop. Even though he'd said he would call, I wasn't counting on it. I'd left Mexico behind as a pleasant dream, another adventure. And now, here I was, sounding like an idiot on the phone, stuttering and giggling. He asked me if he could send me a ticket to come to New York and visit him on the Fourth of July. Without any of my usual hesitation, I said yes.

As the wheels hit the runway at La Guardia Airport, I wondered if I'd lost my mind. *I barely know this man and have agreed to spend a weekend with him at his friend's beach house on the New Jersey shore. What am I thinking?* It was the most spontaneous thing I'd ever done. *He could be an axe murderer … no one will ever find me,* I thought. I hadn't told Stephen or anyone other than Marian that I was seeing him. It was too soon. We'd simply spent a fun day and evening together in Mexico, shared some great conversations, food, drink, a few passionate kisses and phone numbers.

He carried my bags to his car. It was around nine o'clock and the sky was dark at first, but as we pulled out of the parking lot, the sky exploded into a bowl of brilliant colors. "Shea Stadium fireworks," he told me, already becoming my tour guide. One after another, the dazzling, dancing colors streamed harmoniously. I looked at Michael, who'd pulled the car over so we could watch. He looked at me with those black almond eyes and wide grin. "Just for you," he said.

We drove out to the New Jersey shore, to the home of Billy, one of his best friends from high school. A small group of other high school friends were also there and they welcomed me like I was one of them. We swam in the ocean, drank wine, barbequed and talked until the sun inched its way above the horizon. Over the next three days, Michael and I slowly peeled back the layers of our past. We talked about our different childhoods (his seemed like the Cleavers compared to mine), our pet peeves about yappy dogs, infomercials and disco music, and our mutual love of ethnic food and travel. By the end of the weekend, we wondered if we might have a future.

For the next six months, with him in New York and me in Atlanta, we spoke by phone every night, sometimes for hours at a time. It seemed an effective diversion and a powerful anesthetic for my grief. Every two or three weekends, one of us would make the trip to see the other, with little regard for our mounting expenses. I spent all of my extra income on airline tickets. He did the same. Neither of us was earning very much money, but we'd lost our practical reasoning, hungry for each other, full of passion and excitement. Yet at the same time, I felt a sharp pain in my stomach. Thinking it might be an ulcer, I actually saw a doctor. At times the cramps were intolerable. Strangely, they grew worse whenever we were about to be together. All the tests came back negative. "Stress," the doctor said. Stomach disturbances were not foreign to me since my mother died.

The relationship felt like a fantasy, not a real relationship. As the months wore on, it became increasingly harder to be apart and too expensive to be together. I was managing my GI problems, not attributing them to anything in particular. We knew one of us would have to make a move in order for the relationship to progress. He had signed a two-year job contract, so I began applying for advertising jobs in New York. It didn't take long to get an acceptable offer with a Spanish-speaking advertising agency.

Saying good-bye to Marian felt like the untwining of a tightly woven rope. She'd been my life line and now I was letting go. "You should do this, Steph. Go for it," she said, with my interest always at heart. But we both knew what we were giving up. We promised each other visits and calls, but silently knew things would never be the same. After days of helping me pack, she finally stood behind the U-Haul truck that fall morning, both of us waving and trying not to cry.

Michael had flown down the day before to help load the truck and take me up to the Big Apple. When we were at a safe distance, I sobbed like a baby, and I suspect she did the same.

We arrived in New York City on Halloween night, with all of my belongings in tow. The city was a festival of freaks. At a stoplight on the upper-east side near Harlem, painted ghouls danced around our truck, beating on the sides to the rhythm of their boom box music. I could barely keep my jaw from chattering from nerves and cold. The pain in my stomach was expanding and sharpening. I had never lived in a city so electrifying and vibrant. I remembered my crazy subway ride to Sloan-Kettering when I was thirteen.

Happy as I was to finally be with Michael, I knew I had left behind the only place in the world that felt familiar to me anymore. Atlanta had given birth to me as an adult. It was the place where I'd learned to rely on myself and created my own home after losing my mother. I was excited to start a new relationship and experience the thrill of New York City, but I was frightened of shedding a part of myself, a part that I had earned at great cost.

My new job started the very next day. Michael sensed my nerves and the following morning took me out to breakfast, holding my hand like it was my first day of kindergarten. Sitting across the table from me at the Nectar Café on the corner of Seventy-Sixth and Madison, he spoke casually and calmly. I couldn't eat. In addition to my GI problems, I now developed jaw pain every time I opened my mouth. With little awareness of my inner emotional turmoil, it was as if the only language my body had were these symptoms. I was unable to digest my mother's death and was clenching my jaw to avoid speaking of it. My knees knocked together under the table and I wondered if I'd ever adjust to such a big city or anywhere for that matter. I secretly remembered my mother's words and tried to calm myself by chanting, *everything will be all right, everything will be all right.*

A few weeks later, we spent our first Christmas Eve together. As was his tradition, we drove out to New Jersey to his older sister's home. As we were crossing over the Washington Bridge, the city lights glimmered all around me, silently cajoling, almost obliging, me to feel some anticipation and joy. I sat silently, trying to prepare myself for another holiday without my mother. Ever since she'd died, I had silently boycotted Christmas, trying to convince myself that it was just another day. Here I was now, an impersonator, trying to smile and pretend to believe in the miracle of Christmas.

We entered the foyer of the house to find ourselves in the middle of a large, loud group of at least sixty people. Even the most intimate of his family's gathering always amounted to no fewer than twenty people, where the decibel level at any given time was enough to warrant buying stock in an ear plug company. To the degree that my family was fragmented and distant, Michael's was cohesive and overpowering. I hadn't seen my family in years, yet his expected to see us for dinner almost every Sunday afternoon. We hung up our coats and made our way through the crowd to get a drink. I was ready for a strong gin and tonic.

His sisters, parents, brother-in-law, nieces, nephews, aunts, uncles and other relatives all greeted me warmly. For a while, it was easy to get swept up in the chatter and the food was delicious. Like a large Italian or Greek family, their lives centered on each other … and food. Shortly, his youngest sister, made her way over to me and within a few seconds asked me the same question she asked me every time I saw her, "so when is the wedding date?" Michael, now thirty-three, was the youngest, the only son, and the only unmarried one. He was the star and had been a bachelor long enough, according to them.

In the middle of taking a bite of lasagna, I felt my throat constrict and my face flush red with fury. I'd had enough. "The more you ask, the less likely it is to happen, so please stop asking, will you? We'll let you know if and when we decide on a date," I snapped. With her eyebrows raised, she retreated.

While I knew their intentions were good, I was hard-pressed to accept his family's attention and affection, mostly considering them loud and intrusive, and I spent considerable time and energy figuring out ways to avoid them. I felt suffocated and annoyed, partially by their strong presence, but also by the absence of my own family, namely my mother. There was no balance, no representation of my identity and when I was with Michael's family, I was reduced to extreme irritability and a bundle of nerves. They were a large and boisterous group. *Who are these people and what am I doing here?* I wondered. I couldn't wait for the evening to be over.

On our drive back into the city, Michael tried to lighten my mood by singing Christmas carols. Pushed to my limit, I snapped at him too, "You and your family are obnoxious!" and dissolved into a puddle of tears.

Work camouflaged my nerves. The fast pace and glamorous fringe benefits of the advertising world were exciting and distracting. Like everyone else in New York, I worked sixty-hour weeks and weekends. I traveled constantly, making presentations, sleeping in different hotels and entertaining clients at nice restaurants. I was able to lose myself for a while, to hold the mounting chatter in my head at bay. I ignored the little voices that kept asking me what I was doing, telling me that I was lost, that I was going too fast, that I was in over my head, that I needed help. Michael was present to the degree that he could be, but he didn't hear the chatter or feel the confusion that I did. He was happy, finally ready to start thinking about the future. I, however, felt as if I was standing in the middle of a railroad interchange, with six trains converging on me. New relationship, new job, new city, new life, murdered mother and absent father. Michael wanted to help, but didn't know how. When he asked me to marry him, I knew I was in trouble. My mantra had stopped working.

A friend gave me her name, Jill. She was a tall and attractive Jewish woman with dark hair and a soft voice. She knew all about the chatter and the abyss. She had a PhD in them. From the moment I walked into her small and inviting office on the upper west side, she offered me a rope to grab onto, holding her end firm and steady. It had only taken me seven years since my mother's murder to figure out that I could use a therapist.

Jill confirmed what I already knew, that I had to suspend wedding plans or any major decisions, to slow things down, to focus on climbing back up to level ground. Michael was hurt initially asking, "how long is this going to take?" but eventually came around. For over a year I met with her every week, sometimes twice. Thankfully, my work insurance covered the cost. During each hour with her, I slowly emptied out my turmoil, while filling up her waste paper basket with tissues.

Among a hundred other conversations and questions, one day she asked me, "Do you love him?"

"Yes, but I'm afraid of getting married," I said honestly.

"Why?"

"Because I think it'll ultimately fail. Most marriages fail, right? Look at the statistics."

"And what happens if it fails?" she asked.

I didn't have an answer.

"Maybe this isn't about *your* marriage," she said. Strange I'd never made the connection.

"Look. I'm not suggesting that you should or shouldn't get married. But you should be clear. Right now, you seem to be avoiding a whole institution based on a fear that what happened to your parents will happen to you. It's not logical." I sat listening.

"What happened after your mother got divorced?" She redirected the conversation slightly.

I knew where she was going now. "She was killed."

"Are you afraid that might happen to you?"

"Maybe, on a subconscious level," I admitted.

She nodded, then pushed further. "Do you want to have children one day?"

"Maybe, but the thought of it scares me too." Fear seemed to be my recurring theme.

"Why?" She was a clever woman.

"Because, I'm afraid they'll suffer too much. I mean, what happens if I die? They'll be motherless."

"Like you."

"Like me."

"Let's talk about your fear of dying."

Oh God. Is there no end to this? I wondered. "I could. I mean, it happens. Right?"

"How many people do you know who have lost their mothers before the age of twenty?" I couldn't think of anyone else right off.

Layer by layer, week after week, month after month, she gently exposed me to myself, not allowing me to distort reality or side-step rational thinking. She made me walk through the room.

By the next fall I noticed a change in my inner landscape, as if standing in a different place than when I first walked into Jill's office. It was a much more comfortable place. I'd rediscovered my mantra. While still fearful, I was also able to feel optimistic about the idea of marriage and maybe even a family.

Michael and I set a spring wedding date. His mother wanted control of the event, but I knew I had to have it or else be deluged. When she offered her wedding dress, I graciously accepted, hoping to counterbalance any ill will for everything else I had declined. Michael and I planned a small wedding and reception on the Upper East Side with immediate family and friends. Surprisingly, it was important to me to be married in a Catholic church, surprising because I had taken a break from church and all things religious after my mother's meaningless death. Like Stephen, I could not reconcile how an almighty and powerful God could have let such a senseless and heinous thing happen. Despite my bitterness and skepticism, I knew it would have been important to her. As I so often did, I asked myself, *what would she want?* I wanted to honor her. Michael agreed.

I asked Marian and her sister to sing. I asked my half-sister, Annie, to be my bridesmaid, and after doubtful deliberation, I asked my father, while visiting from Hong Kong, to walk me down the aisle. Despite his lack of any other contribution, I wanted him there. And as always, Stephen showed up to support me.

But it was not an easy walk for me, as I also walked hand-in-hand with my mother's absence. Her death had been like a grenade, threatening to sabotage every festivity. If I called forth her presence, I invited the reality of her absence, yet if I could somehow (although impossibly) suppress her, I invited guilt for trying to move on. And my father seemed insensitive to this turmoil in my life. Any possibility of evoking her spirit was squelched when my father convinced me not to invite her sisters, my Aunt Joy, Jessie and Frannie, because it would make *him* too uncomfortable. In search of peace, I acquiesced, a decision I should have known I'd later regret.

Michael in his tuxedo, looked proud and happy. Me in my mother-in-law's dress, felt anxious and bittersweet. I managed to make it to the front of the church. While sitting at the altar, I steadied my nerves by listening intently to the words of the old Irish song Marian was singing. I had trusted her with the suggestion, because her music and voice had always mapped what was in my heart. I let the words and melody wash over me.

> *The water is wide, I cannot get oer*
> *Neither have I wings to fly*
> *Give me a boat that can carry two*
> *And both shall row, my love and I*

At the end of the first verse, I looked over at Michael, tears brimming in his eyes. At that moment, my heart was still a fragile seed, but it was taking root with him, marking a new beginning. For the first time since my mother had died, I could imagine my future.

Twenty-One
Imposter

My mother, a product of the forties, had reveled in being a wife and a mother, until she was no longer a wife and had no means to support herself. Before she died, I'd heard her advice loud and clear. "You need to have your own career and be able to take care of yourself." After she died, her words became like Holy Scripture. Marriage was fine, but the job, the career and almighty security were her silent 11th commandment, always summoned by my wondering, "what would she want me to do?" She had been the voice in my head urging a professional degree and a high paying job.

My first job in New York City was working as an account executive for a Spanish-speaking advertising agency that handled the Hispanic marketing of Coca Cola. I suppose I seemed particularly poised for it since I had grown up in South America, spoke Spanish and had graduated from Emory University, also known as Coca Cola U following a large endowment from the CEO of the company. While I was grateful for the gift of a second language and understood the value of having grown up in a different culture, I often questioned which culture represented my true self. And this job brought this nagging question to the forefront of my mind.

Interestingly, after moving to New York, I spent much of my time back in Atlanta on client trips, since Coca Cola is headquartered there. Except for one other account executive, everyone else in the agency was Hispanic and the primary language spoken in the office and on business trips was Spanish. It often felt like I was not in the United States. I was partnered with an elderly creative director named Guillermo, with whom I was expected to travel to and from Atlanta almost every week.

On one of our early trips, we were sitting around a large conference table with nine middle-aged Hispanic men speaking Spanish, with Guillermo on my right. I was the youngest person and only female at the table, trying to contribute to the conversation, feeling a little out of my league. Yes, I had a business degree, spoke Spanish and had a cultural understanding of Latin and South America, but I was American, feeling almost dizzy by the similarities between these men and my father. My outer self may have registered calm and composed, but my inner self was seated again at our family dinner table in Montevideo, where I was reduced to a bundle of nerves listening to my father's commanding and critical voice. Distracted and somewhere between here and there, I was unsure if the foot rubbing against my right ankle under the table was real or imagined. Then, Guillermo asked with a sly smile, "Que dices muñeca?" (*What do you say, doll?*) All eyes were on me waiting for an answer. My face flushed as I jerked back in my seat, retracting my foot and unsure of what we were even speaking about. I stumbled through the rest of the meeting, not only humiliated by him, but also disappointed in myself for not knowing how to handle the situation. I had gotten a good education and should have been confident enough to stand my ground, yet could not help but wonder, *Why did I take this job? I'm not cut out for this!*

Thankfully, I met Marian, who was still living in Atlanta, for dinner that night. It was a comfort to catch up with someone who knew me so well and get her advice. After a couple of gin and tonics and my recounting the story, she said, "Tell the jackass to cool it or you'll report him to *el presidente*." I loved her strength and knew she was right. When I finally made it to my hotel room around midnight, I noticed my message light was blinking: two messages from Guillermo and one from Michael, who was just checking in as he always did. In the first, Guillermo was obviously drunk, slurring his words, asking if I wanted to meet him for a drink. In the second, he was almost incoherent, asking if he could come to my room. I deleted both and called Michael back to unload my day's events.

"I think you should quit this job. This is ridiculous," he said.

"What if he knocks on my door?" I asked, feeling worried and unsafe.

"Don't answer and call security." I barely slept that night.

At a loss for how to navigate the situation, I wanted to pack it in and go home. But even home was a nebulous place for me. My recurring feeling of being untethered and uncomfortable in so many situations had become an exhausting baseline from which I operated.

When I returned to New York, I asked to meet with my boss, Roberto, another Hispanic middle-aged man. I awkwardly told him what was happening with Guillermo, certain he would do something about it. Instead, he said quite definitively in Spanish, "You're an adult. You need to handle this." Sexual harassment was not yet on the American radar, and certainly not on any Hispanic one. I immediately began looking for another job and gave my two-week notice within a month. Yet somehow, I left feeling like a failure.

In my next two jobs, I seemed to gain my footing, climbing the ladder in the advertising world and enjoying all the perks that came with it: travel, expensive dinners, gifts from suppliers, prestige and a nice salary. I knew my mother would have been proud that I had achieved what she never had. I could tell my father was proud as well. Now living in Connecticut, he'd occasionally take the train in to have lunch with me. We'd meet in midtown at a swanky restaurant and spend an hour or two chatting about Margaret, Heather and Holly, his new assignment with IBM and my latest projects as an account executive at Ogilvy & Mather. On the outside, I looked successful; I was becoming an expert at camouflaging my inner unease, even to myself.

On a four-day business trip to California, after a particularly successful advertising campaign for an airline client, I realized yet again that I was still on shaky ground. It was an appreciation trip, a gift to us by our client, who flew our entire advertising team out to San Francisco for an all-expense paid weekend of wining, dining and adventure. It had been a challenging few months of 60-hour weeks and weekends, but it had paid off. Our group consisted of seven people from the agency and four from our client, all young, energetic, seemingly at the top of our games, mostly single and working well together.

Michael had been patient, even supportive, with my hours and absences from many gatherings with friends and family, and our lack of time together. I felt myself drifting away from him, away from us, sometimes wondering if this must have been how my father strayed from my mother. Work was becoming the center of my life. I was busy and challenged, grateful not to be thinking about the past, or anything else for that matter.

On the last day of the trip, we rented bikes for the day in Napa Valley and set out early for a fifty-mile ride, which included stopping at different vineyards for wine samplings and lunch. I was still feeling woozy from the night before, which involved a lot of drinking, clubbing and dancing until well after midnight. By now, I'd figured out that boozing, flirtations and infidelities were somewhat endemic in the advertising world and par for the course. My direct boss was there and seemed to be carrying on with one of our young, pretty clients, while his wife was back on the east coast looking after their three children.

By mid-afternoon, after two wine samplings at different vineyards, we stopped for lunch. I was feeling tired and ready to call it quits, but we still had another few hours on our return. The chatter was congenial and light, and the drinks kept coming. As we mounted our bikes to ride back, I felt unsteady, yet was unwilling to say anything, always trying to maintain my façade of strength.

Back on the two-lane road, with my heart pounding, sweat beading, and my knees throbbing as I pushed hard to cycle up the next incline, my front tire caught the groove of an intersecting crack in the road, throwing me off my bike, into the air and onto the street. In a split second, just after I hit the ground, I felt the whoosh of a car passing within inches of my skull. The tire of the car tugged at my scalp, leaving a thick tread mark of tar and dirt in my hair. Everyone stopped, asking, "Are you ok?" I struggled to compose myself, dusted myself off and climbed back on my bike, suppressing my tears, until everyone was far enough away. I fell to the back of the line, cycling as best I could with tears running down my cheeks and trying to control my jitters and my bike. It was as if the crack in the road was a symbol for the widening crack in my constructed world. *This isn't working for me,* I mumbled to myself. *I need help.*

Once I got back to New York, I made an appointment with Jill, my therapist, who I'd seen less frequently since getting married.

"It's as if I don't know who I really am and I'm fooling everyone with this successful exterior … like an imposter," I admitted to her in my next session.

"Tell me more," she said.

"I feel like I am a projection of who I think I should be."

"Who do you think you should be?"

"I should be independent and successful," I said.

"Is that who YOU think you should be or someone else?" she probed.

"I don't know," I fumbled with my shirtsleeve. "It's what my mother always wanted for me."

Jill's eyebrows raised. "Why do you think she wanted that?"

"So I wouldn't wind up like her, I guess." *Here we go again,* I thought. "Ok. I get it!"

"What do you get?"

"That I am not my mother!" I knew this intellectually, but her death had elevated her to my patron saint of wisdom. It seemed I was trying even harder to please her in death than when she was alive.

"Perhaps you are focusing on her weakness or hardship as a means of keeping her alive in you. Do you think she would want that for you?" I knew the answer was no. The fact was, I'd already surpassed the wish she had for me. I was a successful career woman making a good income and would not wind up like her.

"Why not concentrate on some of her strengths or talents?" she asked. "Wouldn't that be a more positive way to preserve her memory?"

Like the ancient Greek parable, "The Sword of Damocles," perhaps I had overestimated or mistaken the benefits of wealth and success for peace and happiness. I recalled the story of Damocles, a pandering courtier to King Dionysius, who exclaimed how extremely fortunate the king was that his great power and authority surrounded him with such magnificence. King Dionysius then offered to switch places with Damocles, so that he could taste that very fortune firsthand. Damocles quickly and eagerly accepted the king's proposal. When he sat down in the king's throne, surrounded by every luxury, he also noticed a sword hanging above him, held only by a single hair of a horse's tail. Damocles finally asked the king to be allowed to return to his own life, as he no longer wanted to be so powerful, realizing that with great fortune and glitter also came fear.

I'd never thought of this. *Could I still honor and hold onto my mother, yet de-emphasize the part of her story that did not serve me in order to try and be happy in my own right? And if I could not, what would my future look like?* I knew something had to change. But what?

Coming home from work a few nights later, in the mailroom of our apartment building I saw, as I had many times before, the course catalog for the 92nd street YMCA, a world-class community organization for the arts, located just up the street from us. The headline read, "Art that Changes Lives, Ideas that Change the World." Near the bottom it read, "Over a Century of Creating Space for Innovation, Enlightenment and Personal Creativity." This time I stuffed it in my briefcase and carried it upstairs. After talking with Michael over a glass of wine and Chinese takeout, catching up on our day's activities and doing dishes side by side in our galley kitchen, he stepped into the shower of our tiny 600 square foot apartment. I sat on the couch sipping a cup of hot tea and flipping through the pages of the catalog. I considered, for the first time, courses that might previously have seemed like frivolous meanderings: *Figure Drawing in Chalk, Landscapes with Watercolors, Cooking for Wellness, Ballroom Dancing, Transcendental Meditation, Beginning Pottery, The*

Secrets of Sanskrit, and many more. I enjoyed my job, but needed a way to step out of my tightly constructed, practical and success-driven world. *Pottery it is!* I thought.

Over the next six weeks, I took the Lexington Avenue Green Line directly to the 92nd Street Y every Thursday night, dropped my briefcase at the door and exchanged my dress shirt for one of Michael's crummy button downs, so the clay could splatter any which way it wanted. As each class began, time disappeared when my hands sunk deep into the wet, thick, sticky clay. It felt like an intimate act, where this ground up earth and I became one, where I was safely tethered to terra firma, yet allowed to wander far from the complexities of any earthly pain and hurt. I molded flower vases, bowls, cups and pencil holders. These mementos still sit on shelves, scattered through my home, reminding me of how I learned to unearth some small piece of my epicenter and reshape it into a soul-saving place I'd not visited since my mother died. Each Friday thereafter, while fashionably dressed in my business suits at work, I'd smile at the brown stain left under my fingernails.

Twenty-Two
Training Ground

The waiting room was full. It had taken weeks to get an appointment at Yale University Medical Center with Dr. Sherwin Nuland, a renowned cancer surgeon and author of a bestselling book, *How We Die: Reflections on Life's Final Chapter.* He had come highly recommended for both his brilliant clinical skills and compassionate bedside manner. I signed my father's name at the front desk and took a seat beside him, feeling much like I'd taken a number at the deli counter.

He hadn't looked good for months, complaining of no appetite and a dull stomachache. He'd dropped a rapid twenty-five pounds, and his skin had turned a pasty ashen color. Michael and I had relocated to Florida for a job opportunity and calmer quality of life, and my father's phone calls were becoming more frequent and serious. He'd seen a doctor or two, tests were being run, but there was nothing conclusive. Finally, he was referred to Yale. This appointment with Nuland was the culmination of all the testing, a definitive diagnosis. I flew to Connecticut to accompany him.

It was the thick of winter, grey and cold, but not enough to freeze the drizzling rain. Just the two of us on the highway with me behind the wheel, we drove for over an hour, listening to his favorite Pavarotti cassette and the rhythm of the windshield wipers. We spoke only intermittently and superficially. The ache in my own stomach grew larger with every advancing mile. Margaret, his third wife, had a migraine, saying she was unable to come. Perhaps in denial, believing that through avoidance, she could somehow change the inevitable outcome. Finally, he took my hand, holding it tightly with eyes still on the road.

"I'm OK with whatever I'm told today, Steph. If it's cancer, I want to face this thing head on. No pretending. Okay?"

139

How strange to hear my father being so forthright and brave, unwilling to deny the facts, as he had so often done in the past. This sudden shift in him divulged the gravity of the situation and the ultimate reality we were facing.

"OK, Dad." Was all I could muster.

It had been over a year since my father moved back from Hong Kong with Margaret and their two beautiful baby daughters. My newest half-sisters, Heather and Holly, bore striking resemblances to me, Stephen, Annie, Susie and Carlos. There was no denying my father's dominant gene pool. His Latin traits of dark hair, olive complexion and brown eyes overpowered any significant characteristics from his three wives. Carlos, in typical form, commented at one of our few family gatherings, "We may be screwed up, but damn we're a good-looking family!" He also affectionately referred to Stephen as his "brother from another mother."

I loved spending time with Heather and Holly, perhaps because the age gap between us was too great to feel any jealousy. Even though I was not yet a mother, I felt maternal toward them, enjoying them as I'd never enjoyed other children. When Heather was in kindergarten, I took the day off from work one day. Margaret arranged for me to take her to school and spend the morning. I entered the classroom holding Heather's hand and introduced myself to her teacher. "Hi, I'm Heather's sister, here to visit this morning."

"You mean her aunt?" she said, not so much as a question, but a correction.

"No, actually, I'm her older half-sister ... it's complicated," I stammered. "I hope it's ok for me to stay a bit." I had decided early on not to label, and somehow limit, my feelings for my siblings by using the word "half." Inevitably, though, I had to explain or else tolerate quiet looks of confusion.

"Oh certainly, of course." Her face flushed as she guided me over to Heather's cubby, where Heather was intently unpacking her crayons from her backpack.

Shortly, I was sitting next to Heather, with our bodies leaning in to each other and her soft skin touching mine. In circle time, we listened to "The Very Hungry Caterpillar" and sang unabashedly, as we did the hand motions to "The Wheels on the Bus," both of us smiling ear to ear.

Their innocence and vulnerability drew me in, eliciting a protective response, perhaps from what I unconsciously knew lay ahead of them. It had been over ten years since my mother's death and I, more than any of my other siblings, wanted a relationship with my father. Or perhaps it was need more than want. Regardless, I felt a magnetic pull toward something uncertain with him, and by extension his new family, who seemed to embrace me in return. Although I often felt like the outsider, I must have subconsciously reasoned that some relationship with family was better than no relationship. I kept coming back for more.

The waiting room had the look and feel of last resort. A University Medical Center is where people go when all other avenues have been exhausted, save more holistic approaches or voodoo. When they called his name, he struggled out of his chair. I stepped closer to help him, he took my hand. How could it be that my vibrant and strong-willed father, at only fifty-nine, looked like eighty, so frail and old? The little girl inside me was unable to conceive of him in the grip of something so powerful.

We were led to Dr. Nuland's large and private office, where hundreds of medical books lined the walls and a large mahogany desk full of papers and charts filled one end of the room. It was clearly the office of a brilliant academic and surgeon. We sat down on the other side of the desk, across from his empty seat, quietly awaiting him. All the tests and exams had been done, so we were only here to talk, to hear the final verdict and his sentencing.

On his desk was a picture of him and his family, two dark-haired children and a blonde wife who appeared unrelated and too young to be their mother. Perhaps she was his second and the children were from his first. I was staring at the picture thinking, *My father and he might have some things in common,* when he entered behind us.

After shaking hands and the barest of formalities, he sat down behind his desk and flipped open my father's chart. He laid it on the line. "I'm sorry to have to tell you that the pathology confirms it to be pancreatic cancer. Unfortunately there's no cure, just things we can do to make you more comfortable, Mr. Marbá." The silence was deafening and the room began closing in. Unable to speak, I heard my father say, "How long do I have?"

"I hesitate to say, because everyone's different, but the statistics show, without any intervention, around six months."

More words interspersed with awkward silences; the conversation eventually came to an end. We walked silently to the car, hand in hand. I didn't let myself cry, perhaps because he had never allowed it, or perhaps because I could not accept that I'd soon be parentless.

My father opted for the chemo and radiation, which overtook his life. On one of many weekends I flew up from Florida, I accompanied him for his treatment on a Saturday in December. I covered him with a blanket, as the room was always cold, and made us each a cup of hot tea. Sitting next to him, watching a bag of purple liquid course through his veins, I asked him, "how do you stay so strong?" He leaned over and whispered, "You know I've always been a tough bastard." I'd appreciated his levity and now honesty. Then, more seriously, he said, "I mostly do it for Margaret and the kids, and because I figure I can go through this ordeal in one of two ways: miserably or with dignity. I'm working on the latter." Cancer had softened his hard edges.

A few weeks later, we were sitting in the family room. Me on the floor with Heather and Holly, him still in his pajamas and robe sitting in a nearby armchair in front of a large-paned window where outside the snow was gently falling. Margaret was making hot chocolate in the kitchen. Easter was nearing and the girls and I were making miniature Easter baskets with Play Doh, filling them with tiny eggs, just being silly. Holly made an Easter bunny, a blob of clay with two protrusions for ears and a ball for a tail. Heather, the older, more curious one, asked, "Does everyone celebrate Easter?"

"Not everyone," I said, trying to be the big sister who could explain everything in the world to these sweet girls. Everything except how their father was going to die, how they'd probably never remember him when they were my age, how soon enough, their life would change, how it wouldn't be easy without him and how I always wanted to protect them from all the pain I knew existed in the world.

"There are lots of different religions in the world. Easter is a Christian celebration, for people like us." I sounded like a teacher. "Some people are Buddhist or Muslim. Others are Jewish. They celebrate Passover."

My father sat listening, working a wad of clay on his own. "Look!" he announced. "I'm a Hassidic Jew." When we turned to him, there he sat with a flat disc on the crown of his head, a skullcap, and two rectangular side locks hanging from each of his side burns. "Shalom!" he said, grinning widely to Heather. And to Holly, "Mazeltov!" Mostly out of comic relief, Margaret and I howled at his characteristic and politically incorrect joke.

When he permanently retreated to bed just a few months later, unable to climb the stairs anymore and just a shell of the man he once was, I sat by his bed talking for hours. I never had this kind of time with my mother before she died. It was a different kind of conversation than he and I'd ever had, more honest, more resolute. Time was running out and I was about to lose the father I was just learning to love, the one I'd always yearned for. I finally felt like I could speak to him.

"What happened to you and Mom?" I asked, still confused after all these years.

"I was young, Steph. Foolish and selfish. I thought I needed to be worshipped by a woman. I didn't see marriage as a partnership. Maybe it was my Latin upbringing." This was an attitude I'd seen in many of my male Cuban relatives. An attitude I swore I'd never marry.

143

"Your mother was a good woman." He played with the corner of his bed sheet. "My ego got in the way and I hurt her terribly. I let you kids down." His eyes welled up more these days. He seemed broken. I took his hand, but my thoughts went to my older half siblings. They were the ones who had been let down the most.

"What about Annie, Susie and Carlos? Don't you think you should speak with them?" I wondered if I'd crossed a line. There'd never been much of a connection between them and I still feared my father's rage. But there was no rage left in this man.

"There's so much water under the bridge with them. I don't think there's anything I could say."

"Maybe you should try," I pushed.

He turned his head away. "What's done is done. There's nothing I can do about it now." *How could he still be so proud, or perhaps cowardly, not to ask their forgiveness, to give them the approval he himself had so desperately sought from his own father and been denied? He knew the pain of this first hand.* I stared at the ground, silently disappointed in him and for them. "I have to think about Margaret, Heather and Holly now. They need me the most," he said, as if his heart were not big enough for anyone else. Of all his wives, Margaret was the most dependent on him. Unable to balance a checkbook, pay bills, live on a budget or even keep the house organized and clean, she was in denial of her impending widowhood.

"Can you promise me one thing, Steph?" I felt myself stiffen.

"Can you please keep in touch with them? Don't forget about them. Margaret doesn't have any other family. The girls need you in their lives."

"I'll do my best, Dad," wondering what that would involve.

On my last visit, I sat on the side of his bed shortly before leaving to catch my flight. Heather and Holly played all around us, barely noticing anything out of the ordinary, too young to understand that the end was near, that soon enough he'd be gone. Pavarotti played in the background. I sat quietly holding his hand. "I'm sorry, Steph, for all the stupid things I did, and all the things I didn't." My eyes welled up. I tightened my hand around his. With my throat too tight

144

to speak, I hoped that he knew that the squeeze meant I forgave him, that I'd always loved him despite all of his imperfections. Sadly, I was the only one of his children to whom he apologized, despite the fact that I was the one he'd hurt the least. Like his father, even in death, he still couldn't make things completely right.

As if it were my training ground, unconsciously foreshadowing how I would later forgive Nathan, this was the first time I understood what forgiving could truly mean to me. I was sad to lose my father and hurt by all he'd done and left undone, but some invisible weight was lifted off my back, leaving me grateful for the precious gift of putting things to rest, at least between the two of us. He died three days later.

On a brilliant and crisp fall day, my father's seven children and last wife gathered with others for his memorial service in Ridgefield, Connecticut. It was held at a Congregational Church, because after two divorces, my father never felt comfortable returning to the Catholic church. During the service, my father delivered his final blow to Annie, Susie and Carlos.

A business friend read the eulogy my father helped write before he died. At the very end, after espousing all my father's business accomplishments, he named my father's survivors -- everyone except Annie, Susie and Carlos. All seven of us sitting in the front row were stunned by this omission. Although I had been named, I was sickened with disappointment in him and broken-hearted for my older half siblings. Carlos and Annie appeared stoic, or maybe just hardened after so many years of feeling invisible in their father's eyes. But Susie promptly tumbled out of her pew, ran from the chapel to her car, and broke down in uncontrollable, heaving sobs. Heather and Holly were too young, but Carlos, Annie, Stephen and I followed her out to the parking lot. We stood huddled together, speechless, each one touching Susie, trying to help her catch her breath, supporting her -- and each other. *Had my father simply forgotten to include them? Was he that cruel?* How strange that through his neglect, or in spite of it, he had brought us all together and helped fuel an enduring relationship.

145

Twenty-Three
Angola
(2004)

Gary drives me past the more chilling buildings: extended lock down, death row and the death house. He shares the history of the execution chamber, including the old electric chair, Gruesome Gertie, now housed in the museum just outside the prison. He rattles off statistics about the death row inmates, famous executions, the last execution, issues with the current technique of lethal injection and more. *The ultimate eye for an eye,* I think. A wave of cold and fatigue overtakes me, as I'm reminded that I've spent most of the past twenty years silently bitter that Nathan only got a life sentence, that he should have gotten the death penalty. Because he was high on PCP and potentially delusional, he only got first-degree manslaughter and life with no parole.

That I care at all whether Nathan adjusted here or not, or what his time was like here for over half his life, or why I care about any of this, nags at me. My consciousness of this comes to me in brief flashes, like a lighthouse on a rocky coast. In these flashes, I question myself, my motivation and perhaps my mental well-being. I have gone from not even knowing his name for twenty years to wanting to now know every intimate detail of his life. *What's wrong with me? Can this be normal?* I have felt like a sinking vessel for so long, but now my curiosity rises like one of its air filled buoys, maybe even a life preserver, trying to reach the water's surface. Partially untethered, it repeatedly tries to ascend, but I pull it back. I quietly obsess about why I am obsessed.

Gary's voice reels me in, as he shares a few poignant stories about inmates fighting to be exonerated for crimes they probably never committed. Some are even lifers or death row inmates. "With the help of DNA testing and some very committed lawyers who work pro bono, it's been determined that there are a few inmates who've been falsely accused and convicted. But we uphold the law until we are told otherwise," he says. I vaguely recall reading about *The Innocence Project*, a non-profit organization dedicated to post conviction exonerations of wrongly convicted innocent people through DNA testing. *A noble cause*, I think, as I cannot imagine anything worse than being sent to a place like this for something I did not do, especially for the rest of my life or while awaiting a mandated death. But most prisoners, like Nathan, are here because they deserve to be. They earned every bit of it. Regardless of their innocence or guilt, all prisoners here seem scarred by some large misdeed, mistake or imperfection. Gary summarizes that there are two kinds of inmates here: those who show remarkable perseverance in the face of hopelessness and others who have souls as bitter as bile. I wonder to which group Nathan belonged. Perhaps he belonged to both during different times of his twenty years here before dying. As much as I don't want to consider it, I wonder, *might he have evolved?*

While faith and sense of purpose seem to be a determining factor for hope versus hopelessness within Angola, I realize that the same applies beyond these prison walls. We all need hope to survive. Somehow, the once fixed lines between these men, their deeds, their families and their victims are beginning to feel a bit blurred, drifting into shades of grey. I am not sure if I am simply fatigued and confused, or if something is shifting, even softening, inside of me.

Twenty-Four
Baby Book

I dream my mother is alive. She's moved within an hour's drive from my home and I've yet to go and visit her. I desperately want to, but things keep getting in the way: my children's activities, social obligations and other ridiculous excuses. I'm worried about what condition I'll find her in because I haven't seen her in twenty years.

Her three sisters, my aunts, have been telling me she's alright, but that she won't leave her new townhouse since she had to relocate after Katrina, when all of them lost their homes. They've all relocated, even my dead mother, to be closer to their children. But I haven't been able to reconnect with mine, who now sounds like a recluse. I try calling her by phone, but can't get the number right. I try and try again. I try driving to her house, but the directions are incorrect. I yearn to see her, to look into her hazel eyes, to wrap her in my arms as though we were one person, to tell her how much I love her, how much I've missed her and to introduce her to my daughters, her only grandchildren, who I know she'll adore. She feels so close, yet far away.

At the baby shower for my first daughter, Sarah Jeanne, my husband's family gave me a baby book to catalogue the different stages of her life. It was yellow with blue and pink trim, practically suited for either gender, since we wanted to be surprised. It had spaces for writing and photographic entries beginning before a child was even born. It included the diagram of a family tree and space to record early birthdays, first words and steps, school days and other milestones.

Of the many gifts I received, this one I loved the most, for it reminded me of one of the few treasured artifacts preserved from my own childhood, a similar book my mother had made for me. Mine, however, had a blue cover, now warped and discolored from years of moving and storage units. Despite its tattered condition, it contained many small black and white photographs and hand written notes from my mother.

149

There was a snapshot of her in her late twenties outside in the snow with Stephen and me, around ages six and three, on a brilliant winter's day. We were in Yardley, Pennsylvania, shortly before moving to Puerto Rico. I am facing the camera smiling in a furry blue waistcoat with a white trim hood and a heart appliqué on the front. She is on her knees kissing me from the side, with her hands just under my coat on my rounded belly, as my brother and a friend watch from behind. I presume my father took the picture. Her smile was radiant and her cheeks rosy from the cold -- a mother clearly enjoying a playful moment with her children. In another, more candid shot, taken maybe a couple of years later, my mother stood outside a school bus I'd just boarded for my first day of kindergarten. Wiping away her tears, she waved to me through the window. It wouldn't be long before I knew that bittersweet moment of sending my youngest child off to school in much the same way -- a moment after which I likely would have picked up the phone to call my mother to reminisce and to be consoled. The pages were full of distant memories, a gift from my mother, which, like the silver bell, the miniature tea set and family portrait, made their way into my home years after she died. I treasured these items, as so many things had mysteriously disappeared after my parents' divorce, particularly photographs of my mother.

I began filling the book out months before Sarah Jeanne was born, with all the best intentions of making it a masterpiece for her future enjoyment. But with every picture I pasted in it, every note I wrote, I secretly wondered if I would live long enough to give it to her. It became a living memorial or testament of my love for her, in case she lost me, just as I had lost my mother. My earlier admission in therapy – that the odds of a history repeating itself were unlikely – now felt like an insincere counterargument to the fact that I would die early and leave her motherless. Like a broken record, this song would play in my head over and over again throughout every stage of my children's early lives. With this shadow hanging over me, I took extra care in filling out this book.

I did not anticipate the power that becoming a mother would have over me. That a child would tilt the axis of my already fragile world even more. After my father finally passed away, Michael and I settled into a more relaxed life in Florida. I was no longer traveling to Connecticut every other weekend and when not working, we enjoyed our free time together, walking the beach, barbequing and going to the movies. He began talking about starting a family. As always, he was a few steps ahead of me, eager to get things going. Partly because I often felt flooded by his eagerness and partly because I was secretly terrified, it went in one ear and out the other. Unlike many women, whose clocks were ticking away, mine was barely discernable. We had, however, relaxed on birth control.

When I came out of the bathroom one summer weekend afternoon carrying a positive EPT stick, he was elated, scooping me up, twirling me around, ready to call the whole family. "Let's go out for a nice dinner and celebrate tonight," he suggested, as we had been on an austerity plan with all the expenses of moving and starting a practice. I felt suddenly tentative, almost panicked, just as I had during those early Christmases at my in-laws. I could barely eat that night, unsure if it was anxiety or pregnancy hormones.

Although I was not really aware of it, I suppose I had some vague notion that becoming a mother could be a tricky business for me, given my early loss. Its manifestation, perhaps, might have been seen through my pre-pregnancy ambivalence, my borderline disdain of making a long term commitment, my generalized fear of loving anyone so much that they could deepen the existing crack in my heart. Yet none of this was conscious. It was background chatter, like the steady drone of static. I was clueless about the ways in which becoming a mother would emotionally engulf me, inextricably linking me to my own mother in paradoxical ways.

We named her Sarah, the Hebrew name for noble princess, and Jeanne, after my mother. When we brought her home from the hospital, I stood alone in the shower after cutting off my hospital tags and peeling off my clothes, every muscle aching after labor, the solid weight of swelling throbbing between my legs, hormones rushing through me like the deluge of an opened dike, blood running down my leg. It had been a long and difficult delivery. My body was not my own. I leaned into the towel bar, my head between my hands, shoulders heaving as tears streamed down my face. Here I was, a new mother, desperately missing my own. *How will I know what to do with a child? I'm still a child myself*, I thought. I quietly called to her, evoking her strength in helping me fulfill this new role for which I felt so ill equipped.

Michael's mother moved in for a few days, dovetailed by Aunt Joy. Between them, they taught me how to change diapers, bathe, burp and calm a crying baby. I was able to nap intermittently during the day, in order to regain my strength, knowing Sarah Jeanne was in good hands, probably in better hands than mine. When the week was over, I waved good-bye at the door as Aunt Joy's car pulled away and my eyes filled with tears. Michael's surgery practice had taken him back to work right away. Finally left alone with my new baby, the responsibility of caring for this fragile new life felt like a grand act of juggling joy and fear.

One of the first nights we had her home, I recall a nightmare of me pushing an old-fashioned baby stroller in a park near the top of many stone steps. *I am distracted by something, when all of the sudden the stroller slips from my hands. It rolls toward the steps, as I desperately try to catch up to it. Panic stricken, I watch it tumble downward. Before it hits the bottom, I wake with a jolt.* With my heart pounding, I wonder if people can die from heart attacks from their dreams. I was relieved to awaken and feel Michael next to me. His steady breathing calmed me. Reaching into the basinet at the side of our bed, I pulled Sarah Jeanne's body snug to mine, smelling her baby sweetness, her little fingers wrapped tightly around mine, her soft breath against my cheek. Still mixing up her days and nights, both of us lay dreamily, our eyes locked onto each other. We were two bodies, melded into one. And through the shadows of the twilight I imagined someone else in the room. I felt my mother, peaceful and present, rocking in a nearby chair looking toward us, and heard her silent mantra. *Had she heard me summon her?*

Michael was a confident father, unafraid to handle or be left alone with her. One Sunday, when she was a few months old and napping, I went to the grocery store. Somewhere in the produce section, I began to grow anxious that something was wrong. I omitted half the items on my list and rushed home. When I got there, Michael, who knew me well, saw the worried look on my face. At first he was confused and then lovingly shook his head. "She's ok," he whispered as I stood over her watching the rise and fall of her chest, making sure she was still breathing. His steady calmness helped neutralize my underlying feeling that the other shoe was always about to drop.

One morning, when Sarah Jeanne was already two, and I was nine months pregnant with Hannah, I stood naked in front of the mirror, staring at my belly, the size of a basketball. My eyes traced the darkened line extending down from my navel, expanding out to the blood-rich veins under skin stretched to its limit. My face, fuller now, slightly rounded through the cheeks, my chestnut hair, thick as a horse's mane. Mine was a body in the full bloom of another expected life.

Sarah Jeanne played quietly in the next room, while I readied myself to take her to the park, where I met weekly with some other mothers and their toddlers. Amidst her quiet babble, her self-absorbed contented rambling, I found myself lost in happy wonderment that I had come to this point, that I'd become a woman myself, that I was the mother of one, soon to be two beautiful baby girls. As if standing on both sides of a door, this rite of passage was a paradox of exhilarating joy and extreme sorrow. Already, there were a thousand moments of Sarah Jeanne's young life that I hadn't shared with my mother.

As the babble continued, I glanced into the other room. Always glancing. The nervous habit of a new mother making sure no harm has come to her child. She was holding the phone to her ear now, chatting, mimicking me, I suppose. Pausing, her pensive eyes revealed that someone was saying something back to her. I gently took the receiver from her and said "hello?" There was a woman with a heavy German accent on the other end saying hello back to me. "May I help you?" I asked. "That's what I'm asking you!" she answered. Going back and forth with the woman, I finally deduced that Sarah Jeanne had been pushing buttons on the phone and called a lovely woman in Salzburg, Germany. I hung up the phone, scooped her up, rolled around on the bed, teasing and tickling her, saying "Silly Sarah Jeanne Bean" as she exploded in contagious laughter over and over again. *I should save the phone bill for her baby book,* I thought.

Later that night I told the story to Michael's mother. I'd become accustomed to calling my mother-in-law to share everything from a crazy antic to a high fever. Stephen, now living overseas, had a demanding job, but managed to fly in and out occasionally. Sarah Jeanne was a marvel, but a mystery to him, as he had decided not to have children. Our lives were now on different trajectories. Whatever bubbled up inside of me needed to be shared with someone who also loved Sarah Jeanne, who cherished every new milestone or little nuance. And who better than her *other* grandmother, who always did her very best to bridge the gap. Yet even though I can't remember a single time my mother-in-law wasn't genuinely interested, concerned or amused, I couldn't escape the underlying void of my mother's presence that infiltrated each one of these moments.

And now we were expecting a second. Another girl we were told. Unlike when I was pregnant with Sarah, where I hadn't known how much my heart would grow, this time a persistent fear grew inside of me, like a separate body unto itself. For loving anyone this much was too great a risk. Losing them or them losing me was too much to bear. I wasn't certain I could endure the worry, let alone the loss. Yet I rationalized my fear of them losing me with the comfort of knowing that they would have each other, just as I had had my brother. I always returned to the same story.

At the park every Wednesday morning, Sarah played alongside her friends, running endlessly between the slide, the swing and the tilt-a-whirl. I sat off to the side, on the bench with two other mothers, making idle chatter. It was a comfort to have other women with whom to laugh at each other's baby stories and get ideas from. Inevitably, though, the conversations would steer into incidental places I couldn't go. "My mother took him for the weekend so I could get some rest. When I picked him up, he didn't want to leave." Or, "My mother stopped by with a pot of chicken soup when I wasn't feeling well last week." How easily it rolled off their tongues. These silent moments with friends had occurred ever since my mother died, but now, a mother myself, they seemed to grow more pronounced. I yearned to tell incidental stories, to ramble on casually about my mother doing this or that … how she stopped by to drop off a quart of milk and ended up staying for dinner so she could hear all about Sarah's first day of school. Despite the many years that had passed, the loss now seemed greater in many ways, expanding beyond just my own experience. It was now my child's and my mother's loss as well.

Hannah Joy, who personified her middle name, was an easy and contented baby, adding a new dimension to our family. Like the columns of a house, she balanced us by taking us from three to four, by teaching Sarah to share and by providing me an even greater sense of completeness. How rich I felt to be a typically busy mother. And typical was a welcome feeling, as I so often felt set apart from other mothers.

She was a more physically active baby, crawling, climbing, running and jumping much earlier than Sarah. I held my breath constantly, waiting for the split chin or broken arm. With equal intensity, she showered her affections on those she loved, hugging and snuggling so close that I swear she'd have climbed back inside of me if she could. It was as if she unconsciously sensed my past hurt and was determined to make up for it with her ferocious love. Like an addictive drug, I could not get enough of it.

Not a single day started, especially when they were little, that I didn't wake and feel an unconscious euphoria at the thought of seeing them, sleepy-eyed and serene in their pajamas. And once they had outgrown their cribs, I waited for the pitter-patter of feet against tile, running down the hallway, culminating with a leap into my bed for cartoons and snuggling. "It feels like Christmas every day," I wrote in their baby books.

Between five and eight years old, Hannah went through a period when occasionally, just after reading a good-night story, before lights out and a goodnight kiss, she'd wrap her arms around me like a velvet cloak, overcome with emotion and whispering through her tears, "I love you so much, I don't know what I'd do if I ever lost you, Mommy." My heart would drop like lead, because I knew too well I couldn't promise it would never happen. In fact, in the deepest crevices of my mind, I secretly expected it would.

I hadn't revealed the details of my mother's murder to either of my daughters, but neither had I lied to them. Every now and then they'd bring it up, "How did your Mom die again?" I answered their questions as generally as possible, "She died in an accident at a store," I'd say, reassuring them that it was a highly unusual thing that was unlikely to ever happen again in our family. When they were finally in middle school and still asking, I knew I could not conceal the truth anymore. I told them that a bad man had killed her. "Why?" Hannah asked. "I don't know, honey … sometimes people do horrible things," I said. In the silence that followed, I felt the crushing weight of my own inadequacy, as if I had failed them somehow. I had failed them by not having a better explanation for why these things happen, for introducing fear into their lives, for not being able to protect them from such pain and ugliness. Even after so many years, I felt my throat constrict when speaking about my mother, especially to my own daughters. I wanted to bring her to life for them somehow, but I could not find a way. How could I play the responsible, reassuring adult, when I myself was so unsure? Becoming a mother had been a powerful antidote to my grief and sadness, yet it made me twice as vulnerable to pain and worry.

At her birth, Hannah also received a similar baby book as Sarah. In both of them was a section titled "A Mother's Note." It was a place for me to reflect on our first few years together, their milestones and my impressions of them. In one place of Hannah's, I wrote:

Dear Hannah,

Your middle name, Joy, suits you perfectly. At twenty-two months, you are such a happy baby, always skipping, playing and singing. When you say, "I Love You" unprovoked and smack your lips, I'm amazed by your sweetness. Your curly chestnut hair and big smile are as striking as your affectionate nature. I'm so lucky that you always love to hold my hand, cuddle in bed and sit in my lap. Already you love to say grace at dinner, count to ten and say your ABC's. In addition to being bright, you're very agile and coordinated. I can tell you'll be very athletic or an excellent dancer. I'm so lucky to be your mother and look forward to every stage of your life. I hope that one day you'll be blessed with a daughter as wonderful as you. Then, you'll understand how much joy you bring to me.

I love you.

Mom.

I wrote them each a letter to the best of my ability, but at each sitting, words seemed to fail my truest expression of what their births had given me. As in a highly charged soliloquy, I wanted to say that while my mother's death had broken me, they were the closest thing to wholeness I could have ever hoped for. That they had become my true north, the fixed point by which I could situate all other points. They were my new home. And that because of them, I had been able to travel seamlessly from the deepest sorrow to the peak of renewal a thousand times over.

Twenty-Five
Turbulence

When Sarah was four and Hannah was two, we moved to a larger home on the Loxahatchee River. Living on the water was a life-long dream of Michael's and I was happy to oblige, as we were spilling out of our first home with the addition of two young children.

It had been a distress sale, sold by the estate of a man who had recently perished in a plane crash. The realtor had called on a Saturday morning before the house was even listed on the market, telling us that the circumstances were a little unusual. "This could be very advantageous for you. The family needs to unload it," he said. "A house like this'll be gone as soon as it lists." We'd been looking at riverfront homes for months, but everything seemed out of our price range. But this one sounded interesting, so we left Sarah and Hannah playing at the neighbor's house and rushed over to meet him in front of the cream-colored Mediterranean stucco with a terracotta tile roof. Tucked beneath a serene canopy of hundred-year-old oaks, the house sat on a quiet bend of the Loxahatchee River. We loved it as soon as we saw it, but I was curiously drawn to the circumstances surrounding the sudden death of the owner and his surviving family members. Like a magnet, I was drawn to such stories.

On the red brick driveway outside of the house, we learned from the realtor that the owner, Evan Shattick, had died in a private plane crash the week before. One of his two ex-wives, Marjorie, was settling the estate. She was inside the house, not alone. Three children from the first ex-wife – who lived out of town and were estranged from Shattick – were also here for the weekend, trying to sort through his belongings. Rachel, Marjorie's daughter who had lived with her father in the house, was inside as well. "It's a little awkward, but I think they'll entertain any reasonable offer, if you know what I mean," the realtor said.

I did know what he meant, at least the part about an awkward family of ex-wives, estranged children and half siblings.

159

"A plane crash?" I asked with raised eyebrows. I was distracted from the issue of the house.

"Where?" Michael asked.

"The Bahamas," said the realtor. "Actually ... I have the news clipping if you're interested." He pulled it out of his briefcase, handing it to me.

> *The U.S. Coast Guard reported that the body of Evan Shattick, 57, of Jupiter, FL was recovered from the crash site, Friday, about 44 miles southeast of Freeport Bahamas. Shattick, alone in the private plane, was flying to the Berry Islands when he sent a distress signal about 10:00 a.m.. That signal was relayed to the Coast Guard's Miami Center. A Falcon jet was dispatched and when over the scene, located debris. Soon after, personnel in a Jayhawk helicopter discovered Shattick's body floating near the fuselage. The cause of the crash is still uncertain. Service is set for today, 11:30 a.m. at Parkside Chapel, 1465 Palm Beach Lakes Boulevard. Interment will be at Eternal Gardens, West Palm Beach.*

As if my mind was an aerial camera, I pictured the scene described, just as I had the scene in the convenience store the night my mother was killed.

We entered the house through a small foyer, which opened into the living room, where Evan's family was seated. Marjorie, the ex, greeted us. Then there was Rachel, a fair skinned, dark-haired teen of about fifteen, standing a few feet behind, almost invisible in her mother's shadow. Her narrow piercing eyes stared at us as if we were uninvited guests at a party, intruders. She silently, skeptically, surveyed the situation, not wanting to yield, but after a few moments cast her eyes downward as if forced to submit to the stark realization that everything she felt so certain about was suddenly very uncertain. Something in Rachel's conflicted expression seemed extremely familiar to me. For a moment, I thought she looked like a mirror image of my younger self.

The other family members remained seated, barely looking up, speaking intermittently in muted tones. The air was thick with tension. We stumbled through the formalities of an uncomfortable situation. "I'm sorry for your loss, we're sorry to intrude at such a difficult time." We shook hands with Marjorie, who gracefully encouraged us. "No problem ... please, take a look around." Strangely, I yearned to move beyond Marjorie to speak with Rachel, to ask her if she was okay, to try and reassure her that she would make it through this. I hadn't been much older when I unexpectedly lost my mother.

Michael was drawn to the dense tropical vegetation throughout the property. Mango, banana and frangipani trees nurtured his secret desire to be a gentleman farmer. Sarah would fall in love with the cozy window seat in the den, where she could curl up with a blanket and book. Hannah would immediately take to the old lopsided swing that hung from a giant banyan tree in the back yard, where she could spend hours swinging through warm salty breezes above protected mangroves lining the shore. As for me, I loved the cast-stone fireplace, an uncommon feature in a Florida home and a vestige of a few treasured childhood years when my family lived in Connecticut. For the first time in my life, after so many moves and changes, I envisioned sprouting roots along the water's edge, among peaceful blue herons and lumbering manatees.

The immediate attraction we felt for the home was tempered by my curiosity. Other homes we had seen were sterile concrete structures, with distant and seemingly organized lives living between them. This one had a strong hint of disarray. Dirty dishes stacked in the kitchen, unmade beds, piles of books and papers, partially hung curtains. No attempt had been made to ready the house for potential buyers. I went from room to room, peering into a stranger's life, everything just as he had left it. In his den was his fully rigged, state of the art fishing rod leaning against the wall. I ran my hand along the shiny metal casing of the reel, almost a rounded mirror, then gently plucked the taut fishing line. "He must have been quite a fisherman," my husband said, an enthusiastic one himself. But I sensed something cooler and hardened. On his desk were piles of papers and books, one opened to where he must have left off. Next to that was his Nikon camera with large telephoto lens. His oversized windbreaker draped loosely on the chair. He was a large man, I thought, almost larger than life, passionate about his hobbies, fishing, flying, photography. My father had also been larger than life and passionate about his hobbies: horseback riding, sailing and photography. He'd left me boxes of slides and photos that chronicled much of my past, although he had removed most pictures of my mother after the divorce. My father's pleasure for living was contagious, but often drove him to near obsession, with little regard for anything or anyone else. Evan's musky scent hung in the air. Who was this man, I wondered? So full of energy, then gone in an instant, with no notice, no chance to reconcile bank accounts or personal relations, no chance to say good-bye. I barely heard the exchange of background voices, "... brand new water heater and garbage disposal ... good as new ..." "Hmm ... septic or sewer?" His life, now stilled, was all around me. Wandering through the house amidst the company of this unknown spirit felt oddly familiar to me.

I had walked through my mother's home after she died in much the same way. Unable to comprehend the reality, stunned. She had walked out of her house that morning to go to work, unaware that it would be the last time she'd pull the door shut, turn the key, sealing all of the details of her life inside. Later, after the shooting, the calls, the funeral, I'd be amidst her books, her faintly scented clothing, her perfume bottles, her silver amethyst ring from Mexico, trying to understand that she wasn't ever coming home again.

The asking price was reasonable, but a stretch for us. We made a low, but affordable offer, which was immediately accepted.

When we finally moved in, I felt Evan's presence everywhere, unable to shake the feeling that I was in *his* home. While Michael and the girls slept soundly, I tossed and turned for the first few weeks. During wakeful nights my heart quickened to the sound of a bang, a door closing, a sigh. On edge, I stared at the walls, praying for his peace and my own.

In the following weeks, during passing conversations at the grocery store or while talking with neighbors, I gathered bits and pieces of his life and death. People would often say, "Oh, you're living in Shattick's old house," or "a shame about his accident ... he was quite a character ...," which was usually accompanied by a chuckle or smirk. My neighbor on the other side of the fence knew Evan fairly well. "That was his second accident, you know." Over a few beers on my patio one day he mentioned that Evan had a close call a few years ago when he ran out of fuel, crashing another plane on the sand, just north of West Palm Beach. It had been a harrowing experience from which he only narrowly escaped. The authorities and several others were amazed that he had survived, strongly warning him of his inexperience and recklessness. After the incident he swore he'd take a few more courses and be more diligent with his flight checks. "He never did though. The experience really shook him up, but I also think he kind of got off on it. It was something to brag about. Ego over humility ... the kind of guy who liked to see how close he could fly to the edge. I guess he found out."

At a neighborhood barbeque one afternoon, I met the woman who lived four doors down. "He was a nice guy to neighbors and friends, but not so nice to his family. Every time I saw Evan he had a different girlfriend," she chuckled.

We continued to receive his mail for quite a while. Mostly bills. There had been no time to close out accounts or take care of business. I forwarded them to Marjorie, the ex, until she asked me to stop. Seeing his name on an envelope while leafing through my own mail always gave me a jolt, a forced encounter with the frailty of life. I remembered the week after my mother's death when I returned to college to find the letter from her in my mailbox. It had been so disorienting, as if receiving a message from beyond.

A few months after moving into our new house, my doorbell rang. I opened the door, surprised to see Rachel. She was thinner, frailer than I remembered. Her long dark hair was pulled back in a ponytail revealing her almost perfectly round face, like a porcelain doll, with hand-painted freckles. Her sage green eyes darted from side to side, looking beyond me into the house that was once hers. I invited her in. She stepped into the foyer. Like an awkward child who is called upon after raising her hand in class and suddenly realizes she does not know the answer, I could see Rachel was uncomfortable. With a small forced smile and barely audible voice, she said, "I was wondering if you might need me to baby-sit for your daughters sometime. I have experience with young children."

My daughters, I thought. I hardly knew Rachel and was a bit unsure of her motivation. Yet I felt tenderness for her. I tried to ease her discomfort by taking her number, placing it in my pocket. Gracefully, I said "Thanks for offering, Rachel. My in-laws live right up the street and help out quite a lot, but I'll keep it in mind if they're ever unavailable." After a pause, I asked, "How are things going for you?"

"Okay, I guess. It's been a lot of change."

I told her that I had lost my mother about her age. She didn't ask for details. We kept it simple, spoke about her school briefly and said goodbye.

After she left, I made myself a cup of tea and went out to the back yard to sit on the lopsided swing. I looked at her phone number again. I envisioned Rachel, a young girl like Sarah or Hannah, here under the giant banyan, swinging bare feet toward the sky, wind blowing in her hair, singing among the hibiscus and bougainvillea. Had her father hung the swing for her? Did she miss her room, which now belonged to Sarah? How strange it must feel to see someone else's furniture and belongings in place of hers. Did she feel resentful of her father's recklessness in family and life, or just sad? I remembered the deep empty ache, the inescapable weight of sadness, the disorientation after the death of both my parents. For a long time, no matter what I did or how hard I tried, nothing could dull the ache or fill the hole.

Evan Shattick, I whispered his name. I wondered if he had thought of Rachel in his final moments, just as I had wondered if my mother had thought of me. How lucid is a person moments before sudden death? Was it true that their life flashes before them? Do they worry for their loved ones? Unlike my mother's sudden death, my father's prolonged cancer had given me the precious gift of time, of long overdue conversations, of putting things to rest, of saying good-bye. In the end, his remorse had given me the gift of forgiveness and peace. Rachel had not received this gift and seemed adrift. She would have to find her own way to forgive her father.

As I drank my tea, I wondered about my interest in Evan Shattick, a complete stranger. *What did he matter to me? And why did I care so much about Rachel?* I let the questions wash over me as I swung to and fro like a child. Perhaps Evan was a homonym of my two incalculable losses. His *life* was a reflection of my father's entangled life ... his *death was* a reflection of my mother's untimely and tragic end. Two deaths represented in one. And Rachel? Remembering my sense of familiarity with her the first day we met, it was as if I was looking down the long dark hallway, seeing the shadow of myself as a young girl, vulnerable and shocked in the turmoil of unexpected tragedy. Rachel and I shared an unspoken legacy of loss, of less than perfect families. When we met, she was beginning her long hard journey through grief as I, twenty years later, could see some of the road behind me.

A year after we moved in, I had to replace the washer and dryer. After pulling the old ones out, I found an old photograph of Evan wedged against the wall, covered in lint and dust. After brushing it off, I examined it. In it, he was standing at the end of a boat dock, maybe in the Bahamas. Although it was faded, I saw his hair was messy. His skin bronzed by the sun. He smiled as he held up a fresh catch, about a two-foot Mahi Mahi. I mailed it along with a note to Rachel at her mother Marjorie's home.

> *Dear Rachel,*
>
> *I hope that you are well. I recently found this photograph of your father buried behind the dryer in the laundry room. Although it is faded, I thought you might want to have it. Best wishes to you and your mother.*
>
> *Warmly, Stephanie*

While there were still so many unknowns held within these walls, I had found some discovery within them too. Finding Evan's picture felt like one of many small rites of exorcism for me, of images made real, then released.

Twenty-Six
Foxholes

The impetus to learn about my mother's killer came unexpectedly one day, from an outsider and virtual stranger, as Michael and I attended an informal meeting at an Episcopal church and school where we were thinking of sending our daughters. Raised in different faiths, Michael and I had considered in what church, if any, we would marry, and in what faith, if any, we would raise our children. It had been "church du jour" for a while and this one seemed to be a possible bridge between us. We had settled, somewhat disagreeably, on a Catholic wedding, but now this question of faith emerged again, with children. Feeling slightly ambivalent myself, Michael as usual took the lead. We were seeking a good education for the girls and a place to spiritually anchor our family. We sat in the back of the room, Michael on one side of me, an attractive pregnant woman on my other. I learned she was also a writer. I thought it was a promising sign and liked her instantly. She explained that she had also been raised Roman Catholic and that she thought of the Episcopal Church like a soft drink, Catholic Light.

Within a few minutes, a short stout man named John, with red wavy hair and a rounded nose, stood up to address our group of about fifteen. He was a church member and the head of a prison ministry called KAIROS. He wanted to speak to us about his work at a local men's prison. I couldn't help but secretly characterize John as a holy roller as he paced back and forth in front of us, carrying his small worn Bible between his hands. *He's one of those*, I thought. John spoke of the prison inmates he worked with and the positive impact forgiveness had had in their lives.

"It's amazing to see how some of these men commit themselves to doing God's work after the terrible things they've done. They turn their lives around," he said. I felt myself twinge, feeling viscerally annoyed.

He's talking crap, I thought.

While I basically believed that forgiveness was a good thing for mankind, it was not something I thought much about, except in the occasional case of an argument with a friend or family member or when encouraging my Sarah and Hannah to make peace with each other. I'd never considered forgiving the man who killed my mother. That brand of forgiveness was for extremists who went on Oprah. I had no interest in having a positive impact on a cold-blooded murderer. In fact, I strongly supported the death penalty, silently bitter that my mother's killer had only received a life sentence.

John continued his talk, but my mind drifted. I wondered if my mother's killer ever stopped to think about her or the night of the murder, the moment that changed everything, in his life and mine. Perhaps she flashed across his mind before nodding off to sleep or while eating in the prison cafeteria. Had they made eye contact in those final moments? Did he ever stop to think about her family and what he'd taken from all of us? Or had he pushed her out of his mind entirely, like a bulldozer clearing the remains of a condemned building until it was just an empty lot? I wondered what he'd say to me if he ever had the opportunity.

The rise in John's voice reeled me in. His hands and Bible now resting on his potbelly, he looked up pensively as he formulated his thoughts. "Inmates sign up for our talks for different reasons." He listed them. Some did it for the air conditioning, because talks were held in the only air-conditioned building in the compound and it got pretty hot out there in the middle of the summer. Others did it for the food, because they brought in chips and soda, which was a treat for inmates. Some did it for a change of pace, and others because they thought they could teach *John* something. "But I don't really care what their reasons are," he shrugged. "My goal is to plant a seed. You see, KAIROS has two basic premises. The first is that prisoners who commit crimes deserve to be there -- I mean, some of these guys are just bad to the bone. They don't deserve anything different. But the second is that, regardless of what they've done, they have a right to know God."

I bought into the first premise, but was holding out on the second. *Rights? Why should they have any rights?* And why, I wondered, would John want to waste his time on these criminals?

He continued to tell a story about a weekend retreat several years back, when an inmate confided he had a crime to confess. "I told him I wasn't a priest and that I didn't think he should tell me because I might have to report it." He was in for burglary, but that wasn't the crime he wanted to confess. He persisted, so John let him talk. He told John he had killed a man in a hit and run accident and wanted to get it off his chest. They talked for a long time. John asked him if he thought it was right that the family never knew what really happened. "Wouldn't you want to know why or how someone you loved was killed, left dead on the side of the road?" he asked. The inmate thought about it for a couple of weeks and then went back to John after a meeting one night and told him he had contacted the family, that he was owning up to it -- that even though it meant more time in the pen, he felt better about himself.

I couldn't help feeling skeptical, like I was listening to a used car salesman.

"A few years ago, we had an independent company look at recidivism in criminals who had been exposed to KAIROS as compared to those who hadn't. I'm not trying to toot our horn, but it's interesting. Eighty percent of all inmates released return to prison within two years. For inmates who have gone through our program, it's only nine percent. We feel pretty good about that."

I suddenly felt exhausted and weary. Two decades after my mother's death, as I sat in the back of this room full of people, John was describing the unthinkable. How could I ever forgive the man who had so thoughtlessly and irrevocably changed the course of my life? If he was going to be allowed to live, he deserved to rot in prison.

But John had tapped a deep vein. I struggled to contain unexpected tears, but they flowed out anyway, steady and profuse. I felt a pounding ringing in my ears, a high-pitched scream of sorts. My chest constricted, trying to contain my emotions and embarrassment, unsure of why I was crying. The more I cried, the more afraid I became. And the more afraid I became, the more I cried.

Like many other emotional reactions I had experienced periodically over twenty years since her death, it came quietly camouflaged like the army of an unexpected blitz. These reactions would catch me by surprise, like falling into a foxhole, following seemingly incidental events such as the holidays or a simple lunch with a friend and her mother. I'd wait for the attack to finish, then climb out, a survivor, but fatigued and worn from the ravage.

Thankfully, Michael sitting next to me, and John, facing me from the front of the room, were the only ones who saw me unravel. Afterward, John approached me, concerned.

"Are you alright? Did I say something to upset you?" But I was too undone and mystified to explain myself.

"No, no. You didn't do anything wrong. I think you must have struck a nerve, though. I'll be alright. Thanks," I said uncertainly. I left him with a baffled look on his face. Michael and I rode home silently with his hand on my lap. The experience rattled me, leaving me unsure of what had happened, and more importantly, what was going to happen.

John's talk changed the dial on my radio. He turned it to a new frequency. I couldn't change it back. Articles in newspapers, magazines, shows on television, and conversations with people, all kept circling back to the topic of forgiveness. An unknowing friend even gave me a thought provoking book called *The Sunflower*, by Simon Wiesenthal, a Jew who was summoned from Lemberg Concentration Camp in 1943 to the bedside of a dying Nazi soldier seeking forgiveness for a crime that had haunted him since committing it one year prior. The dying Nazi confessed to having destroyed, by fire and armaments, a house full of 300 Jews who tried to leap out of windows to escape the burning building, as he gunned them down. After asking Wiesenthal for forgiveness, Wiesenthal left the room without speaking to the dying soldier any further. He then posed the ethical dilemma of whether or not he should have forgiven the dying Nazi to the reader. Following his story, a symposium of fifty-three distinguished men and women weighed in on the possibilities and limits of forgiveness. They were theologians, political leaders, writers, psychiatrists, human rights activists, Holocaust survivors, victims of other crimes and their answers fell on both sides of the question. As I immersed myself in the topic and stories of others, I was forced to face my own situation. Unable to block it out, sickened by the thought of it, I was secretly curious. Who was this man who killed my mother? Having been spared the horror of the trial and his excuses, I knew very little of that time or of him. Not even his name.

Over coffee a few weeks later, I spoke with a trusted pastor and friend, Jeannie.

"Forgiving him might be the 'Christian' thing to do," I said, recalling my early teachings and background, "but the hatred I feel is too strong. I don't think I can." After a while, in a slightly awkward gesture, she took my hand in hers. I tried to relax.

"Maybe you should slow down," she said. "Stop trying so hard to work this out *right now*. This is a big one. Try to be patient and calm and trust that you'll know in due time."

I knew she was right. I tried to go about my business. Michael knew I was grappling with it, but was careful not to say too much. Some days the thought of it would come and go quickly. Others, it would linger for a while before releasing me. Occasionally it wouldn't leave me alone at all, like an irritating thorn just beneath the surface of my skin.

But my curiosity had been ignited, now a steady flame. Unable or unwilling to squelch it, I needed reliable sources to fuel it. First, I called Stephen to ask what he knew of Mom's killer. Like me, he couldn't remember much. Then, I called Aunt Joy.

"His name is Nathan Wolfe, honey. He's the one who shot her," Aunt Joy told me over the phone. She had attended the trial back in 1982, seen him face to face. "He went to Angola State Penitentiary with a life sentence. Two other men went there too, with shorter sentences. I think their names are David Anderson and Russell Jones.

I believe Jones was driving the car and Anderson was in the store with Nathan Wolfe." I wrote down their names. After we hung up, I stared at them for a while. Like shadowed figures emerging from a dense fog, seeing and hearing their names began to make them real.

A few days later, she reluctantly sent me the news clippings she had saved from *The Times Picayune* and the *State's Item*. I guess we were all collecting relics of my mother's life, holding onto anything we could of hers, even articles about her death, trying to keep her with us in small ways. She was the headline in section one, page four of the *Times Picayune* on January 16th, 1980, the day after the murder, when police were still trying to figure out details. It took two more days to apprehend her actual killer, Nathan Wolfe, in a stolen car in Texas. Even though it was twenty years later, it felt as if it had just happened. I still found it hard to believe that it was not a dream, a trick of the unconscious. This was the sort of thing I read about other people, not anyone I knew.

ROBBER GUNS DOWN CASHIER

A 48-year-old woman working part-time in an east New Orleans store was killed last night by an armed robber in an apparently unprovoked shooting. Police have arrested one suspect in the robbery-murder of Jeannette C. Marbán who resided at 1103 Chimney Wood Lane, and are looking for two others. During the robbery, witnesses told police, two robbers entered the store while one remained outside as a driver of the getaway car. "The two of them were walking out of the store and one of them was already out completely when the other one just looked back, hesitated and shot as he walked out the door," said a witness.

As police searched today for the remaining two suspects in the death of Marbán, homicide investigators also probed the fatal shooting yesterday of an insurance policy collector at Clara and Third Streets in an apparent robbery attempt. The victim in that case was Ronald Nollen, of Violet.

Marbán was shot and killed at Paul's Package and Food Store, 8201 Chef Menteur Highway. She died of a gunshot wound in the left side of her chest, the Orleans Parish Coroner said. The two holdup men entered the store shortly before 8:30 p.m. yesterday and took an undetermined amount of money at gunpoint before shooting the cashier as they left, police said. Less than a half an hour later, police spotted three men in a compact car. Detectives said the trio's actions aroused the suspicion of policemen, who tried to stop the car at North Galvez and Eads Streets. A brief car chase and then a foot chase followed, in which one man was caught, but two others escaped, police said.

David Anderson, 18, of Moccassin, California, was booked with first-degree murder and armed robbery in the incident at Chef Menteur, and later rebooked with two additional counts of armed robbery. He is expected to cooperate in the apprehension of the other two perpetrators.

Relatives said Marbán was the store owner's niece and Godchild and had been working part-time about two days a week. "She did it to help her uncle out and pick up a little extra money," said Cynthia Mortillaro, daughter of the store-owner, 74 year old Paul Cutrera. Mortillaro said money from the cash register and from a secret hiding place were missing, indicating Marbán had cooperated with the robbers.

Isadore Fisher, a friend of Marbán's, said he was playing solitaire on a stool and talking to Marbán when the gunmen entered the store. One gunman is described as white, 25, about 5 feet 6 inches tall, with a thin build and shoulder length black hair. The getaway driver, who police said went by the name "Sonny," was described to police as white, in his mid 20s, with a thin build and long blond hair. Two revolvers, one believed to be the murder weapon, were found in the compact car from which the men fled.

(Note: after all three were caught, it was Nathan Wolfe who was ultimately charged with the murder.)

In the margins of this article, other news stories of the day were relegated to near insignificance in comparison to my mother's murder. That the world continued on with local election updates, fluctuations in gasoline prices, zoning issues for commercial buildings and weather disturbances seemed trivial, even abominable.

I'd glanced at this same article twenty years earlier, sitting at Aunt Jessie's kitchen table, the day before the funeral. But I was barely able to read it then; it was just blurry ink on paper.

Aunt Joy's hesitation in sending me the articles now stemmed from fear, wondering how far I'd go to learn about my mother's killer, concerned that I'd be endangering myself in some way, unsure of what Nathan might do to me or my family, either mentally or, even worse, physically if he were ever released. In an accompanying note she'd sent with the news articles, she wrote:

> *Hey Honey,*
>
> *Here's what you asked for, but I'm worried about your doing this. You should be careful about who you speak to and what you say and do. This could be a big can of worms.*
> *Love, Aunt Joy*

I held the article in my hands, the paper now yellowed and musty. It felt dirty just to hold it, like I needed to wash my hands. Transported to January 15, 1980 at 8:30 p.m., I became the anonymous witness from the first paragraph in the article, the imaginary observer, the voyeur once again.

I'm walking up and down the aisle in the back of the store, looking for something, when in walk Nathan Wolfe and David Anderson. Nathan is short and slight in frame. Anderson is a bit stockier and a few inches taller. I hear a ruckus at the front of the store, loud voices, a woman's voice pleading, cooperating, saying 'OK. OK.' I hide behind a rack of snacks, but peer out to see her kneeling on the floor. 'Please don't hurt us. Take whatever you want. Just don't hurt us,' she pleads. I see Nathan jerk her to her feet and yell 'open the register and give me the money.' I hear the ringing of the register being opened and watch her put all the money in a plastic bag Nathan Wolfe is holding. He shoves some in his pocket. David Anderson leaves first to enter the car that Russell Jones is driving. Then, I watch Nathan Wolfe walk backward toward the door, still holding the gun, pointing it in her general direction. Then POP, a sharp sound. She stands still for a second, eyes wide open, but dazed and confused. 'I think I've been shot,' she says quietly to her friend standing right next to her. He leaps toward her before her knees give way. He grabs her under her arms as she falls to the floor. 'Nettie,' he says. 'Nettie, Nettie. Hold on.' I hear a car peel away, and then her friend frantically calling 911.

The article held me in a vice, unwilling to let me go. *Why had she not used the gun in her purse? Had it all happened too quickly? Was she unwilling?* I read the article again and again, until I looked at it from every angle, inside and out, forward and backward, until there was nothing left to consider, except for my desperate need for peace of mind.

Later that day, I called the district attorney's office in New Orleans, where the trial had taken place, to request a copy of the full trial transcript. A clerk called me back several hours later and asked if I also wanted copies of the photos and other physical evidence. "What kind of physical evidence?" I asked.

"Mug shots, pictures taken at the scene of the crime, video surveillance from the store ... that kind of stuff ... but you have to fill out a special request for copies of *those*," he told me.

Stunned that I could even be offered these, I took a moment to think. *Did I want to see pictures of her lying on the floor, of her killer's face, or watch a video of her being shot?* Although I had imagined it, the thought of truly witnessing it made bile bubble up to my throat. I knew my limit and was already there. "No thanks. Maybe later. Just the transcript for now," I said.

"Ok. It could take up to three months to receive it, he said. With little or no idea about what it would reveal, or what I'd do with it, I wrote a check for four hundred dollars and drove to the post office. As the envelope dropped from my hand into the drive-through mailbox, I caught myself shaking my head in the rear view mirror, as if acknowledging the irrefutable evidence that I was obsessed. Another day, I contacted the archives of *The Times Picayune* to obtain all of the news clippings ranging from the time of the murder through the sentencing. I even researched Angola State Penitentiary in Louisiana. All this I placed in an unnamed manila file folder on the side of my desk, periodically adding new pieces of information, phone numbers and addresses, slowly developing a mental profile of her killer, Nathan Wolfe. I was an amnesiac retracing the steps of my buried past.

At last I called the prison.

"I'd like some information on one of your prisoners, please. His name is Nathan Wolfe," I asked the operator politely on the phone.

"Are you a family member?" she asked, matter-of-factly.

"No, I'm the daughter of the woman he killed." How strange it felt to say this out loud to someone.

"I can't give any information out on him. He's protected under the Prisoner's Bill of Rights."

"*He's* protected? How interesting. How ridiculous!" I laughed, first indignant, then irate. He's got rights. He's protected. Where were my mother's rights? Why wasn't she protected? Now, my family and I, also his victims, are denied answers, simply left to live in the wake of his destruction.

"Do you want to speak to someone in the Crime Victim's Services Bureau? They might be able to help you," she offered coldly.

"Yes," I said, not knowing anything about it, unsure where I was headed.

She gave me a phone number. I hung up, made myself a cup of tea to calm my nerves and dialed it. I was connected with the director, Jean Wall, a knowledgeable woman with a southern accent and a compassionate voice. She took her time, enlightening me about the prison system, the Board of Pardons and crime victims' notification requests.

"I'm trying to find out about the man who killed my mother," I began. "His name is Nathan Wolfe. There were two accomplices as well, Russell Jones and David Anderson. I'd like to find out about them too."

"I can't tell you anything about them personally, but I can tell you the status of their terms. Give me a few days. I'll look into it."

I hung up the phone agitated. Michael and the girls could tell I was out of sorts that evening. After I tucked Sarah and Hannah into bed, I told Michael, over a glass of wine, what had happened earlier. The phone conversation clung to me like a strong odor. "Are you sure you want to keep doing this?" he gently asked. I secretly wondered about my mounting preoccupation with all of this and my powerlessness to leave it alone. He was my voice of reason, but was also tolerant and supportive.

When Jean Wall called a few days later, I was in my office and took notes, trying to understand everything she was saying. "Let's start with the two accomplices, David Anderson and Russell Jones. They've been released from the penitentiary after serving shorter sentences because they copped a plea bargain by turning in your mother's killer. Jones was released in 1987 after serving five years, and Andersen was released in 1994 after serving twelve. They were both released before their terms on good behavior."

I was sickened to think that they were now free. *How good could they possibly be?* They were hardened criminals, burglars and accomplices to murder.

"As far as Nathan Wolfe, he's still here. He requested a pardon almost five years ago, but was denied. In the state of Louisiana, a pardon is the only non-judicial way in which a life sentence can be reduced, thereby creating the possibility of an inmate's eventual release from prison." My head was reeling, trying to keep up.

"After an inmate files a request for a pardon, it has to be approved by a board at a hearing. Even if that happens, the Governor finally has to approve it. It hardly ever happens, honey. But he's entitled to request one every five years. So that would be right about now." Suddenly, I felt like a character in a movie, in a race against time, trying to prevent the release of a cold-blooded killer.

"Now?" I said, almost choking. "Can you tell me if he's asking for one now?" I stood up and began to pace five steps in each direction within my small office.

"By law, we've got to notify the victim's family before an inmate's hearing, so they have the opportunity to represent themselves. I see here we notified an Isadore Fisher five years ago. He's the named contact on our crime victims' notification form."

Isadore Fisher? I hadn't heard his name in years. He had been a good friend to my mother, wanted to marry her, in fact. But she

177

wasn't interested in him that way. He was not as intelligent, handsome, worldly or as interesting as my father. He was a simple man, not well spoken or well read. But after the divorce, the loneliness was crushing and my mother was grateful for the companionship and all of his attentiveness. He was the one with her in the store the night she died. He was the one in whose arms she drew her last breath. He was the one who identified her body for the coroner, testified as a witness at the trial and appointed himself the family contact with the Crime Victims' Notification Bureau. But it had all been too much for him. It was his undoing. After the funeral, we lost touch. I heard that he'd had a heart attack a few years later. Aunt Joy had told me she thought he died of a broken heart.

"Isadore Fisher is dead," I said. "How do I change the contact to my name?"

"I'll send you the form. Just mail it back."

Feeling depleted, like I needed to drink a large glass of water, we spoke a little more. I stumbled through my undefined and confused intentions for the call and thanked her for her time. Near the end of the conversation she added, "Honey, let me just give you this number, in case you ever need it. It's the chaplain's office at the prison. You might find it helpful." I wrote the number down, tucked it in my growing manila file, and filed it in my cabinet between "Client Research" and "Letters of Intent" for many weeks, until the next time I came across it, as if it were calling my name.

So Nathan Wolfe had requested a pardon and could request another now. I knew Jean Wall said it hardly ever happened, but there was at least some possibility, no matter how small, that he could be freed. Infamous corrupt Louisiana politics could hardly guarantee that justice would be served. And in my mind, this changed everything. The only thing I could think was that there was no way I could forgive Nathan Wolfe if there was any chance that he could be set free. In fact, my rage and hatred seemed to be deepening, settling like a squatter in my soul.

This time, I was *trapped* in the foxhole and was unable to climb out by myself. At my wits end, I phoned Jeannie, my pastor friend, once again relying on her wisdom. We talked for quite a while.

Actually, she listened as I rambled. After a while, she cut me off. "Maybe you should define forgiveness. What does it mean to you?"

I muddled through a series of meaningless phrases and finally gave up. "I have no idea."

"Maybe, then, think about what forgiveness is *not*. How about we say, it's not forgetting. It's not reconciling. It's not condoning the act. It has nothing to do with him being released from prison. In fact, you should fight to keep him in. How about we say that forgiveness simply means you unburden yourself of anger and bitterness and no longer wish him harm. Justice yes, but not harm. Just think about it for a while."

Her words stilled me, settling the murky water in which I had been vigorously treading, almost drowning, helping me regain some footing and clarity. I wanted to float, to rest, but there could be no rest until I did everything I could to ensure Nathan Wolfe's full life-sentence. Only then could I see clear to any possibility of peace.

According to Jean Wall, a letter to the Pardons Board and the Governor of Louisiana, Mike Foster, would help insure against his release. So I drafted a heartfelt letter and sent it certified to both of them the next day.

May 9, 2000

Dear Governor Foster:

I write to you in reference to Nathan Wolfe (DOC#00101151), who sought a pardon in 1995 for the killing of my mother. I understand he was denied, but that he'll be eligible to seek another hearing this year. I believe you consider these requests carefully before making a pardon and would therefore like to offer my feelings for your consideration in this matter.

It would be impossible to explain the devastating impact the killing of my mother has had on my family and me over the past twenty years. Nathan Wolfe took much more than the life of one victim the night he murdered my mother. He also victimized three sisters, two parents, my brother and me, not to mention many close friends and relatives. It has taken me the better part of my life to try and cope with the effects of Nathan's act. Not only did he take my mother in

179

the prime of her life, but also he took away my youth, my family's peace of mind and our happiness. I was a teenager when this happened, but recovery from it will never completely end.

I now have two children, who will never know their grandmother or their heritage in a tangible way. Instead, they only have a story of a very special woman who would have loved them more than life itself. The effect of Nathan Wolfe's deed continues.

While Nathan may be repentant and remorseful for his actions, which I hope he is, he'll never feel the deep and scarring wounds he left on so many lives. I feel compelled to say that any reduction of sentence would cause severe emotional and mental distress to my family and me. We cannot cope with the idea that he would ever be released. In essence, a pardon or reduction in his sentence would be another devastating event for us. I feel, at the very least, my family and I deserve the peace of mind in knowing that justice has been served and that we will always be safe from him. Our lives have already been shattered once. I beg you, please don't let it happen again.

Thank you for considering my opinion prior to any decision to grant a pardon to Nathan Wolfe. I must trust in you.

I wish to remain anonymous to Nathan Wolfe for the safety of my family and me.

Sincerely,

Stephanie Cassatly

I sent the letter certified, but never received a response. I sent it to ease my mind, to convince myself that I had some control, to try and silence the frantic chatter in my head. As it turned out, I didn't need to send it at all.

Twenty-Seven
Tangible Evidence

Sitting at my desk one afternoon, the house quiet until Sarah and Hannah arrived from school, I heard the thump of a heavy box being dropped at my doorstep by the mailman. The return address read, Criminal District Court, Parish of Orleans. I knew what it was.

Like bills from the tax collector, I let it sit unopened in the foyer, walking past it day after day, unconsciously avoiding its mysterious contents. *Later, when I have time,* I told myself. But it called me relentlessly, drawing me in, until finally, several days later when I was home alone, I sat cross-legged on the floor of my living room and removed the contents. The box contained over four hundred sheets of trial transcripts, fastened into three legal-sized folders, titled "275873, Nathan Wolfe." Tangible evidence. My mother's murder on paper.

While I flipped through the pages, the scent of stale and airless years of storage burned my eyes. Even still, I could not look away. My mind sporadically latched onto disparate and surreal facts. Aunt Joy had previously told me that Harry Connick, Sr. was the prosecutor. And here he was, his stamped letterhead, interspersed between all the details of her murder trial, which I had successfully avoided for two decades.

Flipping farther along, my eye caught the autopsy report. I couldn't breathe, as I stumbled like a cripple, word after word through the description of how the bullet had penetrated my mother's body at the first rib, following a swift path from the right subclavian vein, to the aorta, through the left pulmonary artery, into the left lung, and then exiting through her back, all resulting in a massive left hemothorax. No bullet was recovered. In the coroner's report, she was described as a well-developed, well-nourished white female, about five feet six inches tall, weighing one hundred and forty pounds, with a scalp of light brown hair, hazel green eyes and

181

red painted fingernails. The coroner knew nothing about how many times those hazel green eyes had embraced me or how many different colors she had let me paint those nails. He knew nothing about how beautiful her hair looked in a French twist or how she struggled to be slim. She had been reduced to just another stiff on the table. As an echo reverberates off the walls of a canyon, these written words bounced around the inside of my skull, screaming intimate details of violation, first by the murder and then by the autopsy.

Then, there was Nathan Wolfe's hand-written voluntary statement pleading his case in flawed English.

> I, Nathan w Wolfe, have the right to remain silent and stop any questionig at any time. But I voluntarly waive these rights to tell my side of the story of what happened in my own words. I just want to help myself in this charge for murder and robbing at this time. I Nathan w Wolfe, and sonny (Russell's nickname I presumed) and David was in a Datsun car. We went by the store to see what it looked like. David said let's go rob it. Sonny parked the car in a Traylor park out back. Then me and David walk to the store. David went in first and pulled the gun and said give me the money all of it. So the lady started getting the money out but she was to slow so I Nathan w Wolfe went behind the counter and help get the money to hurry up and get out. Then David told her to give him a carton of Malbor ciggrett's and went out first. I was backing out with the gun up in the air but not ponted at any one. I was looking back at the door and it went off it just went off. I did not mean for it to and then we left and got in the car were sonny was parked and left. I did not go in to hurt any one I could never hurt any one I have'nt got it in me. I have never hurt any one in my life before. I did'nt wont to do it in the first place. But i see what it got me into now. I am verry sorry. Plese plese help me. I'm not this kind of a person to rob and kill some one.

> Nathan W Wolfe 1-25-80

Although he claimed never to have previously hurt anyone, Nathan had killed another man just the day before, shot him from inside the Datsun, while the man stood on the side of the street. When Nathan was later confronted with this charge, he claimed that he was hallucinating, thought that the man had stolen money from him. With the advent of this second charge, Nathan and his lawyer must have decided to request a lunacy hearing. In fact, I found the psychiatric report declaring Nathan Wolfe of sound mind and body. In this report also, I learned he was homosexual. The defense had made an unsuccessful attempt at an insanity plea.

Other sections of the file included the list of jurors, followed by pages of cross-examinations and testimony from everyone involved: the witness in the store, the detective who handled the case, the first responder paramedics, and the two other accused men. Then there was the plea bargain by Anderson and Jones, which pointed the finger at Wolfe, affording them reduced sentences for ratting him out. Lastly, there was Nathan Wolfe's final verdict of first-degree manslaughter, his sentencing to life in prison with no possibility of parole and then, of course, his useless appeal. The die had been cast.

Five hours passed. I had barely moved. My neck ached from hunching over and my stomach vacillated between hunger pangs and nausea. It was time to pick up Sarah and Hannah from school. I packed everything up and stuck the box deep into my closet. On my way out the door, I walked past the hallway mirror and saw the dark shadow of my face, devoid of emotion or expression, like someone under heavy sedation or even paralyzed. I had been struck numb.

As if surfacing from deep waters, an hour later I sat in the brilliant sunshine on a tennis court watching Sarah take a lesson, while Hannah snuggled on my lap eating a snack and swinging her feet as she downloaded all the lovely and trivial events of her day. Finally, she asked, "What did you do today, Mommy?" *I am living two separate lives*, I thought, and then constructed a fictitious day of work and errands. It was becoming increasingly harder to speak to Michael about all this, let alone the girls. I did not want to worry them. Ultimately, this was my private journey to travel. I had to do it alone without dragging them down with me. Thankfully, the risk of Nathan Wolfe drowning me was counteracted by my ordinary daily activities with Sarah, Hannah, and Michael. Making lunches, tennis and swim lessons, birthday parties, barbeques, trips to Home Depot, reading in bed together at night were my life-saving buoys.

The next day, as I'd done for the many subjects in my newspaper articles, I leafed through the manila file folder containing all of my research on Nathan Wolfe. I wanted a profile of the man who took my mother from me. I wanted to know everything about him, to be an expert. I wanted to control everything about him. I wanted to own him. But what I didn't realize then was how much he owned me.

In reality, I knew very little about Nathan, just some vital facts from the trial documents. He was five years older than me, stood only five feet eight inches tall, with mousy brown hair and dark brown eyes. Never having seen a picture of him, he began to take form in my imagination, inhabiting my dreams and most private places of my mind. Thin and gaunt, with long hair, sometimes he'd come to me as a stalker or a rapist, trying to harm me or my children, terrorizing me to the point that I'd wake in a pool of sweat and then have insomnia. Other times as a friend or lover. My subconscious was ignited. Just as a writer creates a despicable or demonic character for one of her novels, tending to him, nurturing him so that he can truly exist on the page or in the reader's mind, authenticating the story and justifying the final epiphany, I assigned physical attributes to Nathan, conjured his tumultuous past, imagined what he was doing in prison at that very moment. Like a victim of Stockholm's Syndrome, where a captive in a hostage crisis, over time, becomes sympathetic to her captor, I felt strangely intimate toward the man I hated most in the world. I was living in polar extremes. At some undefined time and place I silently moved from not wanting to know anything about him to wanting to know everything I could. Who was he and what was his story?

Nathan's identity was born from a few facts on paper and my deep unconscious, a place where only I could go. In this dream-like place, where facts and fiction blur, his story unfolded.

I imagine Nathan's parents were young and poor when they met. Within a couple of months she became pregnant. After a quick and unceremonious marriage at the courthouse, their daughter was born healthy with a pleasant disposition. His income was just enough to support the three of them, but not after he found his way to the casinos on weekends. Soon enough, Nathan's mother had to go back to work, while the neighbor watched the baby. In the beginning, Nathan's father appeared smitten with his daughter, but after a few months, he was more interested in sleeping, eating, working, having sex and gambling. He was faithful to his wife, but she was lonely, even when he was home.

When Nathan's mother became pregnant a second time, it spelled trouble and they both knew it. Nathan was born on September 22, 1955. His father distanced himself even more. His mother was exhausted, struggling to keep things together. She began drinking, trying to quench her thirst for all that was lacking in her marriage.

Unfortunately, neither she nor her husband was smart enough to prevent the third pregnancy. Nathan's little brother was born sickly and frail. Nathan, now four, was already a handful running wild and independent, yet he sat on the curb each afternoon waiting for his sister to walk home from school.

A pivotal event took place when Nathan was six and a half. His father, as usual, was away. It had been an unusually difficult day. When Nathan's mother finally got all three to bed, she began drinking, as usual. Passed out on the couch, she tuned out everything in her life, including her children. Unfortunately, she didn't hear the baby in the throws of an acute asthma attack. In the morning, hung over and half asleep, she found him curled up in his bed, ashen grey and clutching his chest.

Not only was this the unraveling of Nathan's mother, but of the rest of the family as well. Nathan's mother was plagued with guilt. As if her self-loathing weren't enough, her husband was ruthless in blaming her.

Nathan, at eight, was a slight and scrawny kid. He began hanging around a tough group of boys, mostly older than him. When he was only in second grade, he successfully conducted his first robbery. One of his friends dared him to go into a diner and steal something. He took the challenge, like an initiation rite, to impress them. Leaving the others outside to watch through the window, Nathan stepped into the diner and up to the counter. He ordered a soda from the waitress and scanned the restaurant. When a woman sitting next to him stepped off her stool to go to the restroom, leaving her purse wide open, Nathan could hardly believe his luck. He swiftly grabbed her wallet, paid for his soda and headed for the door. He walked outside and into an alley, as the other boys followed, giving him a high-five and patting him on the back. Nathan felt ten feet tall. They opened the wallet and pulled out twenty-five dollars, tossing the rest in the dumpster. They spent the rest of the evening at the local arcade.

At home, there was nothing but dissension. His mother drank and when his father was home, he was abusive and mean. Both Nathan and his sister kept to themselves. When he was just sixteen, Nathan quit going to school. No one, except his sister, seemed to notice. Conversely, school was the only constant thing in her life and she surmised that it would somehow benefit her in the long run. Perhaps she had a teacher that counseled her. She tried to convince Nathan to do the same, but he would hear none of it. He was busy trying to support his expanding booze and drug habit through petty theft. At eighteen, when his group of ill-fated hoodlum friends suggested a road trip to New Orleans one weekend, he said, "What the hell," and took off for The Big Easy.

Nathan was attracted to the seedy lifestyle of the French Quarter. It was easy to blend in there, where the drugs and booze were plentiful. Over the next few years, he led a marginal life, moving from one place to the next. His mental and physical condition deteriorated as his paranoia and confusion increased. Desperate to feed his addictions, eventually he started turning tricks with other men. The money was steady, enough to support his cocaine and heroin habit. In his downward spiral, he also began robbing bigger and better things, like cars and small stores. He had lost touch with his family. His sister graduated high school and went to work, helping support their mother.

The next time Nathan saw his sister was in prison, after committing his final crime, the murder of a faceless woman, a cashier at a convenience store somewhere on the outskirts of New Orleans. When his sister was called and notified of his sentencing, she scraped enough money together for a Greyhound bus ticket to Angola. This was the last time she ever saw Nathan. At first, she would write and even send care packages containing cigarettes, magazines and money, but over the years her communications dwindled and he was left alone to live the marginal life he had earned himself, a life penned up with other hardened criminals.

How did I develop this profile of my mother's killer? Was it real or imagined? I spent weeks poring through four hundred pages of trial transcripts, reading testimonies, depositions and hand-written letters to his attorney, all the time wondering what caused him to do what he did at 8:30 p.m. on the night of January 15, 1980. I had made myself a powerful cocktail, my own version of Nathan's story, mixing a few facts with my ignited imagination.

Twenty-Eight
Katrina

I was cooking dinner when the evening news came on. The girls were in their rooms doing homework after having just gone back to school. Hannah, in 6th grade, and Sarah, in 8th, were becoming more independent. South Florida news during this time of the year always tracked weather, since we were in the middle of hurricane season. Whenever something was brewing in the Atlantic, I paid attention. The Gulf of Mexico, not so much, unless it was near New Orleans, where my aunts, Joy, Jessie and Frannie, still lived.

Living on the coast in Southern Florida, we had been through enough hurricanes in sixteen years that we knew the drill: fill up gas tanks (with cars lined up fifty deep and wrapping around the block), stock the kitchen with non-perishables and bottled water (with store shelves picked clean), fill bath tubs and sinks (and any other available containers), board up windows and doors (with multiple trips and long lines at Home Depot), batten down all exterior objects, including the boat to the dock, and hunker down exhaustedly for a hurricane party (usually a long day or night) with whomever we chose to ride out the storm. Depending on the strength of the hurricane, clean up afterward was often even more tiring. Among the worst we experienced were Hurricanes Jeanne and Frances, the year before Katrina. Both starting as tropical depressions off the coast of Africa and following almost the same trajectory, their eyes made landfall within a few miles of us only three weeks apart, which only added insult to injury. Wind speeds of up to 145 miles per hour, billions of dollars in damage, no electricity or air conditioning in sweltering 100-degree heat and countless other obstacles left us wondering if we were under a state of siege and if Florida was still a place we wanted to live.

The news this evening was from the Gulf. It had almost become routine that if there were storms brewing in the Atlantic, my aunts would call me, and if they were in the Gulf, I would call them. The conversations of, "Have you boarded up? What's your plan? Call me

189

when it passes," were always the same. As I turned my attention to the news, I knew this one would be a challenge. The Mississippi River had always been a threat to New Orleans and Louisiana, including Angola, where Nathan was. Over the years, my grandfather had told us stories of how he worked with other men to secure the levees near his home and how high the river could rise. In its usual form, New Orleans balanced anxiety and the nonchalance of *"Laissez les bon temps roulez"* (Let the good times roll). When Mayor Ray Nagin publicly announced on national television, "Ladies and gentlemen, this is not a test, this is the real deal," I called each aunt to check in, while I watched with increasing concern as Katrina moved ashore. "We're ok here, honey. Not to worry. We know the routine," said Aunt Joy. "I'll call you after it passes."

I expected it would take a day or two until I heard they were all right, since phone lines always jammed after hurricanes. Unlike other hurricanes though, the unfolding events during and after the storm were beyond comprehension. Images of devastating flooding and destruction kept me, and all of America, glued to the television screen. The Mississippi River and its levee breaches would strand thousands of men, women and children on roof tops or in the Superdome for days and weeks on end, collapse bridges, wash away homes and buildings, leak oil and toxic chemicals into entire neighborhoods, carry bodies (both humans and animals) amidst miles of debris, and invite looting and lawlessness to rule the streets. Even the National Guard, Army Corp of Engineers and curfews could not contain the situation. Words like "catastrophic," "ground zero," "mass exodus," "hellish nightmare" and "cataclysm" were in every news headline. Even though street signs were under water, my knowledge of the neighborhoods where my aunts lived and how stubborn they were to leave their homes made the panic rise up inside of me. If they were alive, they were certainly in deep trouble. There would be no deliverance from this one. I called my cousins, who lived out of state, to see what they had heard from their mothers. No one had any information.

I spent a couple of anguished nights and days thinking my aunts had perished. *What did they do when the water came in? How afraid must they have been?* They were too old to climb onto a roof. They could never survive the heat, stress and peril of it all. Joy lived on the edge of the Ninth Ward, one of the hardest hit areas. My mother's old home, near Jessie and Frannie, was completely under water.

After three days of continuous calling, I finally got through to Aunt Joy. I could hear the rise in her voice as she told me that just hours before fifteen feet of water rushed in, against her will, she, her husband, two of my cousins and their families had fled inland to Baton Rouge without packing anything, even extra clothing or her diabetes medications. She was holed up with four other families in a stranger's apartment and sleeping on a floor. As far as she knew, Frannie and Jessie had stayed in their homes. She sobbed like an orphaned baby, paralyzed and hardly made any sense. Hours later, my cousin, Kim, in Ft. Lauderdale, called to tell me she had finally reached her mother, Frannie, who was with Jessie in a town called Covington. They'd crossed Lake Pontchartrain at the 11th hour to go to a friend's house on higher ground. They were stranded, but alive. After all they had been through, my three stubborn and resilient aunts were still alive.

My cousins (outside of Louisiana) and I began a highly charged telephone chain. In what felt like a small miracle, we arranged to have all three of them and my uncle flown out of Baton Rouge together four days later. They arrived at Ft. Lauderdale airport looking haggard, in shock and in tears. I joined my cousins as the next generation to step in and help their parents, just as I would have done if my mother were still alive. I felt transported, almost disoriented, as I vicariously connected to my mother through my aunts. Yet, as always, I still yearned for it to be her instead of them, even if it was to help her through a natural disaster.

The plan was for Frannie to live with her daughter in Ft. Lauderdale, Jessie with her daughter in Arizona, and Joy and her husband with us, until they could move back to Louisiana near their children. They were a tight trio, never having lived more than a few miles apart. As if they hadn't already lost enough: first their childhood home, then my mother, now their adult homes and finally each other. I couldn't help wonder if this wouldn't finish them off.

While Katrina had forced me to take a break from my obsession with Nathan Wolfe, on some level it deepened it. There was a silent and dark part of me that pondered the poetic justice of New Orleans, murder capitol of the world, nearly being wiped off the face of the map. Ever since my mother's murder, I couldn't help but feel that New Orleans was nothing but a corrupt and evil place. I had illogically translated my hatred for Nathan to an entire city. I did not necessarily believe in a vengeful God; in fact after my mother's death I questioned the existence of one at all, but my deepest subconscious likened Katrina to Noah's flood in Genesis, where all the sin and filth of the world was eradicated. I knew, of course, this was irrational and could not be shared openly, because the pain and suffering of so many good people, like my aunts, was palpable and devastating. Katrina, for me, seemed to represent a strange dichotomy that vengeance and compassion could somehow coexist.

The thing about natural disasters is that they reduce everything to the lowest common denominator: food, shelter, health and clothing. Over the next month, I drove Aunt Joy and Uncle Don to insurance agents, FEMA (Federal Emergency Management Agency) and Red Cross centers, doctors, pharmacies and thrift clothing stores. They had been wiped clean. The neighborhood where they lived was condemned after their house had filled with black sludge from a leak at a nearby chemical plant called Murphy Oil. Even months later, when they were finally allowed in, they had to wear Hazmat suits to dig through the rubble. Not a single thing could be retrieved from their house before it finally had to be demolished.

Sarah, Hannah and Michael and I did our best to make them feel at home in the absence of their own. The girls took up a collection at school and our local community reached out in amazing ways I never would have imagined. People who didn't know them lent a car, bought them clothes and handed them cash. One afternoon in the grocery store, I ran into a friend, Beth, who I hadn't seen in a long time. I told her what was happening. That night I received a phone call from her husband, Pete, who sat on the board of a local church (not ours).

"Steph, Beth told me what happened to your family and we want to help." He explained that since the tragedy, they had been trying to contact churches in New Orleans to see what they could do, but that no one returned their calls.

"The message machines are all under water, Pete," I said. "I doubt they are getting your messages."

"Your family members are exactly who we've been looking for. Can we meet?" he asked.

Within a matter of weeks, they gathered two complete homes of new and used furniture, appliances, dishes, utensils, lamps, linens and more: one for Aunt Joy and Don and another for my cousins who were still in Louisiana. They even committed to driving two loaded trucks to wherever they found new homes. This would certainly help them reconstruct their lives.

Aunt Joy cried a lot during those weeks and months, overwhelmed alternatively by a sense of loss and gratitude. I tried to comfort her and say the right thing, imagining what I might say to my own mother, but words often escaped me. It was a matter of just listening and holding her hand. "I've never been on the receiving end of so much. I've always done the giving," she said humbly. We were humbled as well. For as many hurricanes as we had been through, we could not fathom the idea of walking out of our home with the clothes on our backs and never coming back.

While I fell into bed exhausted every night, dreams of my mother were vivid. In one, she told me that she was moving and that I'd have to visit her in a different place, but she didn't know where yet. In another, she thanked me and told me she'd always love me. Perhaps because we were beginning to take more and more care of Michael's aging parents, there was something gratifying in finally being able to help my family, particularly Aunt Joy, who was the closest woman in the world to me next to my mother. At least I could do for her what I could not do for my mother.

After Katrina destroyed their homes and their lives, Jessie and Frannie relocated to small places near their daughters in Arizona and Florida. Joy found a small place just outside of New Orleans near where her children had relocated. As if she had only been on loan to me, I needed to return her to their care. When the moving trucks from my friend's church in Florida pulled into her new driveway in Metairie, Louisiana late one afternoon, after an eleven-hour drive from Florida, she called me crying again. "Honey, I just don't know how to thank you." The truth was that I felt the same way.

Twenty-Nine
Sacred Numerology

That my mother was killed when she was forty-eight years old was a silent benchmark, a point of reference from where I measured all things. It hung over me in the form of vague apprehension through most of my fourth decade, not so much like a gauntlet, but as a matter of fact. I would not surpass her age when she died! On more occasions than I care to remember, I calculated such things as how old the girls would be when I died at forty-eight, my life insurance payout so that Michael could retire and stay home with the girls in my absence, when and what experiences we should have so that they would all remember me after I was gone. While math was never my strong suit, I was always able to quickly calculate the difference from any of my ages to forty-eight, as if forty-eight were the only fixed value worth measuring from. I had unknowingly become a believer in numerology.

I never intentionally voiced these inner ruminations about my mortality with anyone, for fear of being called superstitious. Every so often, however, something would slip out to Michael or a friend. After a pause or a look, I could tell that they were taken aback, as if I was a pessimist or doomsayer. The fact that some people lived long enough to have grandchildren, let alone great grandchildren, was a wonder to me. Secretly, I knew I would never be included in that group.

To a lesser degree, I was also aware of my father's more natural cause of death by cancer. Since I knew the odds of being shot like my mother were unlikely, I somehow merged my parents' two deaths into one (her age and his illness), as if I could design or customize my own demise.

To kick off the decade, Michael planned an amazing and memorable fortieth surprise party for me. It was in a rustic beach shack, with reggae music, great decorations and food, drinks and about forty of my closest friends and family. Stephen even flew in from Mexico, where he was now living and working. It was a complete surprise and I was overcome with emotion by seeing people who'd flown or driven from near and far. Stephen saw my tears first and stepped forward to hug me tightly, just as tightly as I had hugged him so many years ago in the church sacristy during my mother's funeral. I clung to him just as I had then. Despite all the time that had passed, the geographic distance between us, and our different lifestyles, we still tried to protect and show up for each other. It was an unspoken bond, unfortunately born from pain, but one that could not be broken.

The entire night seemed an amazing feat. I reveled in being alive, laughed and danced until my feet hurt. Later that night, lying in bed in Michael's arms, I felt tremendous gratitude that I had been lucky enough to witness this celebration, to feel so much love while still alive, as opposed to being honored at my funeral. Even in light, there was always a shadow side.

Not surprising, in my early forties my stomach issues returned with a vengeance. As I began to lose weight, I became increasingly worried that I had pancreatic cancer like my father. Recalling every detail of my father's early symptoms, I had test after test and went from one unsympathetic doctor to the next, all of whom told me there was nothing wrong with me. Yet I was certain there was. I took antacids for two years to calm my stomach, but this did not settle my mind. Although I said nothing to anyone, I was secretly certain I was dying and wondered if I would even see Sarah or Hannah graduate high school.

As my forty-eighth year approached, I became increasingly more anxious and graduated from pancreatic cancer to breast cancer, after finding multiple lumps in my breasts. Following numerous mammograms, ultrasounds, MRI's, aspirations, biopsies and even a recommendation from an overly aggressive surgeon for a mastectomy, Michael and I went to Moffit Cancer Center to get a complete evaluation. The lumps turned out to be benign cysts and nothing to be alarmed about. Yet, even as I received a clean bill of health, I still doubted I would see Sarah and Hannah graduate college. After all, my mother never saw me graduate college, as I was only eighteen when she died. I would have to live into my fifties to see them graduate. With each advancing year, I held my forty-eighth birthday as my private deadline for when my luck would run out. I lived under the shadow of death, as if going to doctors might be some sort of talisman to outmaneuver or ward off my inevitable ill-fated odds.

The year I turned forty-eight, Hannah took a class in mythology as part of her high school freshman curriculum. We were sitting at the breakfast table one morning discussing her upcoming test on Edith Hamilton's *Mythology: Timeless Tales of God's and Heroes.* Like my mother had done with Stephen and me, I always asked questions as a means of engaging with my daughters, and also helping them learn the material by having them explain it to me. She rambled on about the different gods and their myths: Zeus, Hera, Poseidon, Demeter, Artemis and Moros.

"Who was Moros?" I asked. Although I was no expert, he was the only one I'd never heard of.

"The god of impending doom," she rattled off.

"Really?" My interest was piqued.

"Yeah. Even Zeus was afraid of him."

"Why?"

"Because Moros represented negative destiny and was the only force that Zeus could not alter," she said confidently.

"Sounds pretty hopeless," I offered. "I think you know your stuff," I said about the test.

After she finished eating and retreated to her room, I picked up the book that she left on the table to read more about Moros. His siblings, Thanatos and Ker, represented the physical aspects of death—Ker was the harbinger of violent death, while Thanatos represented a more peaceful, passing away. *Hmmm,* I thought with no hesitation. *According to Greek mythology, Ker took my mother and Thanatos my father. Which one would take me?* I wondered.

If the mortality of Moros wasn't enough, a few weeks later I sat at my kitchen table one morning writing an article for the newspaper. As I gazed out to the river for a few moments to gather my thoughts, I noticed about fifteen black buzzards convening on my back patio. Soon, fifteen became about twenty-five, which then became about thirty-five, or too many to count. I'd never seen so many birds. I called Michael, who was in the other room, to check it out.

"Interesting," he said.

"Ominous," I countered.

"There's probably just something dead out there."

"Maybe it's a sign that something bad is about to happen," I said.

I knew black buzzards were an omen, a metaphor for death. He affectionately rolled his eyes. To assuage my sense of dread, I walked into my study and pulled my father's *Audubon Field Guide to American Birds* off my shelf to look them up. An avid bird lover, he'd given me his copy before he died. When I looked them up, I learned that they feed on carrion and sometimes even kill live animals by pecking, biting, wing-pummeling, and foot-grappling. They are often found on highway margins eating road kill, as well as picking through dumpsters. They nest in dark cavities like caves, hollow trees and abandoned buildings. Their flight style is distinctive: soaring high above scanning for food, with strong wing beats followed by short glides, giving them a bat like appearance. They have no voice box but grunt and hiss when agitated. *I'm ridiculous*, I thought.

On the actual day of my forty-ninth birthday, Sarah, Hannah and Michael orchestrated a special celebration. Michael had done the shopping, Sarah (an excellent and precise cook at 17) made the dinner, and Hannah (more artistic in sensibilities at 15) set a magnificent table with candles, flowers, a nice tablecloth, and even my mother's china and stemware, which I seldom used. And because I was an excellent master of disguise, they did not realize the significance of this particular birthday. I had reached forty-nine, privately surprised I was still alive. Unsure if it was the wine or hormones, a profound feeling of relief, but also disorientation overcame me. *What do I do now?* I wondered. I hadn't really considered life after forty-eight. I had surpassed my mother's age and had not -- and now could not -- have my mother's fate. Everything hereafter would be a bonus, yet this incredible realization of my separateness from her felt strangely sad, almost like losing her all over again. Before my mother died, I never looked at her as my mirror image. Afterward, however, her physical, psychological and emotional attributes became mine. I had become her living manifestation. Yet now that I was living beyond her age, I had no frame of reference for how to live my own life. I would have to learn. I felt a strange sense of freedom, yet also uncertainty of how to navigate within a different world, as if I had been suddenly exonerated from a death sentence and released.

Feeling a need to thank Michael, Sarah and Hannah for my special dinner, I raised my glass for a toast. "To life and new beginnings," I said with tears in my eyes.

"Oh Mom," Sarah teased. "You're such a sap."

"We love you, Mom," said Hannah.

"We should cook you dinner more often," said Michael.

For my fiftieth birthday, a decade I never thought I'd see, my good friend, Hilda, a successful attorney who also dabbles in sacred geometry, gave me a book on interpreting the meaning of numbers. When I looked up the number forty-eight, I was surprised to find that it represents that a cycle or phase will soon be coming to an end, with rewards coming from work well done. "This end or conclusion will lead to auspicious new beginnings and opportunities, which will bring blessings and rewards of many kinds into your life," it read.

Thirty
Notice of Release
(2000)

I dream I'm in the mountains hiking by myself. I come upon a cliff that drops sharply into a canyon. I walk cautiously to the edge, glancing down a vertical 1,000-foot drop, then quickly retreat to safety, ten feet in from the precipice. A few moments later, I inch closer, lingering a little longer at the edge and then retreat once again. There is something beautiful at the bottom of the canyon, but fear keeps me from taking a longer look. I yearn to see it, though. The back and forth continues and each time I linger longer and retreat less, until I can finally see the bottom clearly, without any trepidation. Down below I see a person sitting on a rock, resting, dangling her feet in a stream. I realize it is my mother. She looks up and sees me. She smiles and waves. After a moment, she stands up and disappears into the thick brush. I stand at the edge a moment longer, interested, but assuaged, no longer curious and satisfied by what I have seen. I retreat from the cliff, continuing on my hike.

There was nothing special about the morning when, once again, the door shut behind Michael and the girls bound for work and school. I sighed with relief after the morning rush. I had a few hours before an interview scheduled for a newspaper article. The house was quiet. I walked into the study with my cup of coffee, lingering at my desk, which contained a pile of paperwork. My unnamed manila research file on Nathan Wolfe lay to the side. I sat back into my chair and flipped the file open, reviewing all of my scribbled notes and numbers I hadn't seen in weeks. *I'm obsessed,* I thought. *For what?* The chatter in my head had been relentless and I'd been listening to it for so long. Tired and worn out, I had no idea how to silence it.

As I casually leafed through the pages, a piece of paper fell out. It was the number of the chaplain's office at Angola which Jean Wall of the Crime Victim's Bureau had given me months earlier. I stared at it for a second and simply picked up the phone to dial the number, with no thought of what I'd say. A man with a soft voice and Cajun accent answered. "Chaplain's office, Father La Beauve speaking."

I hesitated. "Hello. My name is Marta."

I felt ashamed of lying to a priest, substituting my middle name. I was too afraid to use my first, though, for fear of being traced. *Only a partial lie,* I thought. "I'm calling to inquire about one of your inmates who killed my mother twenty years ago. I wonder if you could help me."

Now he hesitated.

"Let me ask you, what is it you want to accomplish?"

Oh my God, I thought, feeling reckless, *what have I started?*

"Well," I sank deeper into my chair, like a lead weight. "I'm considering … thinking about … trying to find a way to forgive him, but I don't know if I can," I stumbled. "I guess I want to find out from him what happened that night and whether he feels any remorse." I felt myself beginning to perspire. "I'm afraid of being identified, in case he's ever pardoned."

"Does it make a difference if he feels remorse?" he asked.

My head felt heavy and clouded.

"I'm not sure," I said. *What does remorse have to do with it?* I wondered. I had imagined extreme scenarios a thousand times over; him as an unremorseful and threatening lunatic, ready to kill me too, if only given the chance, a real Charles Manson type, and then, him as a truly repentant and sane individual, tortured by his deed, wanting to make amends. Needless to say, I wished for the latter, because it would certainly be easier to forgive such a person. But I had no way of knowing and felt, somehow, that it shouldn't drive my decision. Yet deep down and honestly, it mattered.

"This is a very brave thing you are attempting, my dear. You are unburdening yourself and walking in the path of our Savior."

I'd never been much for religious chatter. It inevitably made me uncomfortable, but I couldn't deny my early Catholic upbringing as a hidden force in all of this.

"Let's talk about how exactly I can help you. Would you like me to serve as a mediator?" His soothing voice calmed me. He had that special gift that certain people have, emitting almost a sonic vibration as though he truly loved me without even knowing me.

"Maybe … I think so … OK," I said, surprising myself. I stood up and began pacing.

"And how shall we do this?" he asked more pointedly. "Would you like me to deliver a letter from you?" I felt my stomach tighten at the thought of something so tangible between us, as if her killer could touch me through a piece of paper. Father La Beauve interpreted my silence. "Or perhaps you can simply *tell* me what to say and I'll personally deliver the message to him."

My stomach relaxed slightly. "Yes. Maybe that would be better," I said.

"I think it would be best if you were very specific as to what I should say. For instance …"

But I interrupted him with a burst of unexpected clarity. "How about if you say, 'the daughter of the woman you killed in 1980 is trying to forgive you. Do you have anything you want to say in return?'" It sounded so simple, to the point and not totally committed. He repeated it back to me. "That's it," I said.

"Let's do this," said Father La Beauve. "Give me his name and DOC number. I'll find out where he is and go to him with your message. I'll need a week. Can you call me next Friday night at my home, say around 8:00?"

"Yes, that sounds fine. Thank you." I gave him Nathan's full name and DOC number. He gave me his home telephone number. I didn't give him any additional information. When I hung up the phone, I sat down, realizing I'd perspired through my shirt. I had actually done it. Breathing quickly, I thought, *what have I done? What if he's released and comes after me and my family? What if he wants more communication? What if I'm not really ready to forgive? What if, what if, what if?* I wept, choking on my own anxiety.

Twenty years had been a long time. But the following week seemed even longer. It stretched in front of me like a two-lane road heading into the horizon, where the end would never come. I kept myself busy, working, cooking, shopping, cleaning, anything to keep in motion, trying not to think. But at night, with my head on the pillow, that's all I could do. I thought of every possible scenario, mostly worst case. The panic would rise up, throbbing in my chest and head. Feeling almost manic, sleep was nearly impossible. And if I managed to doze, it was fitful and fractured.

Michael and I spoke intermittently about it, but nothing he could say or do, including his gentle embrace during my sleepless nights quelled my nerves. He finally just let me be and listened when it bubbled out of me at different points, knowing that it had to play itself out.

In my frailest moment that week, I once again called Jeannie, my trusted coach throughout this process. Pleading for reassurance, I asked, "What if I've opened Pandora's box? I'm worried for the safety of my family."

"Steph, this is something you've been thinking about for a while. It isn't an impulse. Why don't you sit back and see where it takes you. I don't think you or your family is at risk. Give it some time, girl. It's out of your hands now."

I turned down an invitation to dinner that Friday. "We can't get a sitter," I lied. What was I to say? "I'm speaking to a priest about my mother's murderer?" Murder is a grisly word that always made people uncomfortable. A real conversation stopper: "When I was eighteen my mother was murdered." It was the kind of information that people were initially fascinated by, but then, wanted to keep at arm's length.

The day was orchestrated around the phone call that evening. Michael came home early to work on a small used boat we purchased to explore the Loxahatchee behind our house, a brackish river extending into the Everglades. Sarah and Hannah, full of excitement, were helping him out on the dock. I called them in for an early dinner. At the table, Sarah and Hannah spoke of incidental events at school,

Michael chattered casually with them. I moved the food around on my plate, tuning in and out of the conversation. After dinner and dishes, Michael lured the girls back out to work on the boat, offering me the space and time I needed. I watched the girls skip toward the water while holding his hand, feeling grateful for how clueless and happy they were. I returned to my study, switched on the light, closed the door and sat at my desk, which was piled with individual stacks of work projects; I had tried to be productive that week, but mostly shuffled things around, making no real headway on anything. I took a deep breath before dialing. Father La Beauve answered the phone.

"Ah yes, Marta. You're calling about Nathan." I'd forgotten my pseudonym. Time and space disappeared as I sat motionless, hardly breathing, as if watching a spellbinding movie. "After we spoke on Friday, I located Nathan in the prison. He resides in a minimum-security camp. Angola, as you probably already know, is a maximum-security facility, so he's not considered much of a threat and I'll explain why in a moment." As if the movie was now playing in slow motion, he continued. He'd gone to Nathan on Saturday morning, never having seen him before. "I don't think he's a Catholic and doesn't attend the service I lead every Wednesday evening in his camp." Father La Beauve introduced himself to Nathan. After a few brief words, he delivered my message, just as we'd agreed. Then he asked if he had anything he wished to say in return. "Well, perhaps you can imagine that after twenty years he was taken aback ... in fact he was speechless. After a few moments, he said he needed time to think about it. I told him I'd be back in touch with him in a few days."

Father La Beauve continued. "The following Wednesday when I went to his camp to do my usual service, he was there for the first time. I saw him sitting in the back of the room. After I finished, I went to where he was sitting and we spoke. But before I tell you what he said, I need to tell you something important, my dear. It's what I mentioned before, about him not being a threat to you." Father La Beauve, almost whispering, said, "Nathan is dying. I believe it's cancer, or AIDS. He doesn't look well. In fact, he can't even stand up.

I'm struck by your timing, my dear. That over a twenty-year period, you call *now*. A year ago, he was not sick and might not have received your message so openly. Six months from now he'll likely be dead and you would have missed the opportunity to do this. It only confirms my faith in the workings of a Holy Spirit."

Of all the scenarios I'd imagined, it never crossed my mind that I'd be forgiving a dying man. In that moment, I realized that things were unfolding just as they were intended, according to a plan over which I had no control. I was merely an instrument of something far greater than myself. Trembling, with tears streaming down my cheeks, I found myself smiling, even laughing. I'm sure that Father La Beauve heard the muffled, yet uncontrollable, sound of my simultaneous laughter and crying. I felt self-conscious about my conflicting emotions, mostly the laughter, wondering how I could be laughing at the news of a dying man. Was I that angry and vengeful? But it was something entirely different. It was the realization that for the first time since 1980, I no longer felt anger or vengeance, that I had nothing to fear and that I had been blindly working toward this moment for twenty years, fighting it all the way. *Is this forgiveness and peace?* I wondered.

He continued, "Nathan wishes me to convey how grateful he is for your call. He said he's turning his life over to God and preparing for the end. He also asked me to tell you how deeply sorry he is for what he did. He said that he could never make an excuse for it, but that it was a very bad time in his life, that he never intended to kill anyone, that he was out of his mind on drugs. He asked you to convey his deepest regrets to the rest of your family."

And so I sat there, not knowing what to say. My clothes were soaked, as in a baptism, from perspiration and tears. I asked Father La Beauve if he thought Nathan would be seeking a pardon to be released from prison. "No," he said. "After so many years, the men in his camp are his only family and he wishes to live out whatever time he has left with them." Still at a loss for words, I thanked Father La Beauve and hung up. I sat at my desk and allowed the tears of relief and maybe even sadness. Then, as if a window had been opened, a cold air blew in. The hair on my neck prickled. I felt my mother sitting next to me for the first time since she died. Not in a dream at the bottom of a canyon or in the distance. But right next to me, with her arms wrapped around me. This was what she had wanted all the while.

The next day I sent Father La Beauve flowers and a note that read, "Words cannot express my gratitude. Sincerely, Stephanie Marta Cassatly." He told me later that he was teased by the rest of the Chaplain's office – a Catholic priest receiving flowers from a mystery woman.

~~

On Saturday morning, two days after Christmas, a simple white envelope containing a letter addressed to me arrived from Angola State Penitentiary. It read,

Notice of Release

Pursuant of Department regulation No. C-1-007 and your request regarding Nathan Wolfe, this office is required to advise you of the inmate's release. Subject expired on December 23, 2000.

I stood in the driveway holding the letter to my chest. I closed my eyes to the warm sun, the stilled chatter in my mind, thinking about the word "release." Quiet, steady tears streamed down my cheeks freely. My heart was both heavy and full. We both had been set free. So many years of grieving my mother. How strange now to grieve her killer, for the life he never had, the disastrous choices he made, and the love he probably never felt.

Sarah called me from the dock. "Come and take a ride with us, Mommy." Michael and the girls were waiting for me, ready to take a ride up the river on the boat they had been refurbishing. The last coat of paint was finally dried. I smiled, wiping the tears from my face, and put the note in my pocket to walk toward them.

Thirty-One
Angola – Point Look Out
(2004)

Nearing the end of my tour, we finally arrive at Point Lookout Cemetery, a serene plot of land at the base of the Tunica Hills. "This is where many of our inmates are buried. Funerals in the prison are solitary occasions, most often attended only by those assigned to burial duty," says Gary. He continues to explain that those buried here have died from either state-mandated executions, diseases, old age, or all too often at the hands of other violent inmates. Angola inmates make the coffins and there is a horse-drawn carriage procession to bring them here. Warden Cain believes that after serving full life sentences for their crimes, inmates must celebrate finally going home. There is a white fence that surrounds this green pasture where hundreds of white painted crosses stand lopsidedly in the ground. Their only adornments are small metal plates with just the date of death and serial number of the inmate hammered into them. I ask Gary why there are no names. He explains that ghoulish characters previously vandalized graves of notorious criminals. Notorious or not, these are the graves of banished men, of lifers who committed such horrible crimes that even in death, no one will have anything to do with them. It would seem that death would be a relief, a release from the half-life they've led inside this place.

I step out of the van feeling the still, humid air. A gentle rain has begun to fall. When I called the prison, four months after my conversations with Father La Beauve, to check if Nathan was still alive, I was told that Nathan was in the last stages of his cancer, confined to bed in the prison Hospice program. Preparing for this final stage of my tour, thinking my story will soon be finished as I stand at the foot of my mother's killer's grave, I close my eyes.

I imagine him right in front of me, the shell of a man. With deadly pale skin and wounded brown lips, his eyes are two deep hollows. He lies propped up on a pillow. 'This is Nathan. Nathan, you have a visitor,' says an imaginary nurse to both of us. When he sees me, he nods his head, but his mouth remains fixed, almost frozen. Strangely, I'm not afraid. His eyes follow me as I move to the side of his bed.

'Hello, Nathan, I'm Stephanie,' I say, using my real name, because I know there is nothing to be afraid of anymore, that he'll not be leaving this bed, except to be buried here in Point Lookout Cemetery. He nods and makes an unintelligible sound from his mouth. I strain to understand. The invisible nurse translates. 'He says, hello.' He is no longer a monster, just a dying helpless man.

Gary interrupts my thoughts to say, "when you called to arrange this visit, we thought he was buried here, but after going through the roster, we find that he is not. I apologize for the confusion."

I looked up slowly, not comprehending, stunned. *What? Not here?* I have traveled all this way to see the grave of the man who killed my mother. I have even brought a small medallion on a chain to place on his white cross as a final and orchestrated gesture of his and my final peace, of his and my final release, as if I could actually write my own ending to this story with this act. It's the medal of St. Dismas, the patron saint of prisoners, which I purchased the day before I left Florida in a place called Holy Land, a local Christian curio shop. I'd researched Dismas, like I did everything else for this journey, as one of those obscure saints in the Roman Catholic Church. He was one of the two thieves crucified beside Christ, the penitent one who asked Jesus to remember him, while the other mocked him. The woman in the store had led me to a rack of many small drawers, maybe a hundred in all, each containing small medals for the most popular of the 10,000 Catholic saints. There was one for every occasion, like a Hallmark greeting card.

But I am derailed, realizing this story that I thought was over, still has a missing piece. I do not have everything I need to fully envision or write my ending, to control the final outcome. Nothing so far, from my mother's life and death to forgiving her killer, have I been able to envision or control. Although I have made all these plans and driven all the way out here to this seemingly Godforsaken place, I have the

210

sensation that I am just a passenger on this ride, that instead of me writing this story, this story is writing me.

"Where is he then?" I ask a bit too loudly.

"I thought you might ask me this," he says graciously. "All I can tell you is that his body was released to his next of kin. I'm sorry, I can't release any personal contact information." Even in death, prisoners seem to have more rights than their victims.

With this new development, suddenly I am mystified by the possibility that someone cared enough to do this. His sister, his parents? I'd imagined that he had been abandoned and forgotten. That someone might actually have loved him suddenly widens the circle of others he might have hurt beyond my family and me.

Gary drives me back out through the gates of Angola to my car. The thought flashes through my mind that the only way Nathan was able to exit through these gates was in a box, and I am leaving as a free woman. Thanking Gary for devoting his afternoon to me, I leave Angola with St. Dismas still in my pocket and return home to Florida, where I bury it in the bottom drawer of my dresser, near the envelope containing my mother's high school diploma, death certificate and other documents, the dresser upon which my mother's graduation photograph still sits. With most questions answered, only this one remains. I wonder if I will ever be able to completely finish this story.

Epilogue
(2015)

I am cleaning out my study and come across my old manila file folder. It's been fourteen years since I opened it. It seems like another lifetime. Sarah and Hannah are away at college now, and I teach writing at a university. Stephen and I keep in touch regularly by phone and occasional visits; Michael has retired from his surgery practice and started another career. We are empty nesters now, a label I am wondering if I like or not.

Although I rarely think about Nathan anymore, who requested his remains is a loose end I have mostly ignored. But looking at my old notes, my curiosity about this final question bubbles up inside me. I wonder if Gary Young is even still at the prison. After all, people move. Things change. I write him an email, remind him of my visit years ago and ask again, on the off chance, if he can tell me who requested his remains. Surprisingly, he writes me back, not with a personal contact, but the name of the funeral home where his remains were sent. That's the best he can do. He tells me that the few prisoners that are not buried in Point Lookout are frequently sent there. It's the closest funeral home to the prison. *I guess every business needs a market niche*, I think.

My interest is suddenly sparked again. I decide to call the funeral home. The owner, a kind man, but also a businessman concerned about legalities and privacy rights, confirms that he does in fact have a client contact name to where the remains were sent. I want to reach through the phone and grab the paper he is looking at, but I cannot argue with his reasoning to withhold the contact name from me. "Our clients want closure," he says. *Me too*, I think. Still, I beg, plead and cajole. Having told him I'm a writer, I say, "If you can't share the contact information of where his remains were sent, can you at least please act as an intermediary for me? I need to finish this chapter of my story"... *of my life*, I think. Secretly, I know that I have only imagined Nathan's past, constructed him as a pathetic, lost and unloved soul, perhaps because it was easier to forgive that kind of person. But now, I might have the opportunity to know the truth of who he was. If I know who might have cared for him, who his family really was, what his childhood was really like, what brought him to that fateful day, perhaps I can more fully humanize him and completely release him, I try to explain. Finally the owner agrees to forward a letter from me to the name he secretly holds in his files. He actually asks for two copies of my letter, as he has one name but two addresses and is unsure which, if either, is still viable. After all, it's been fourteen years now. People move. People die.

That night, I pour myself a glass of wine while Michael is away on a business trip and curl up on the couch to write the letter as best I can. At first it is daunting to try to write something so personal to an anonymous person … to encapsulate who I am and what I want. Surprisingly, it flows out easily and smoothly. Somehow, it's not about me anymore. Perhaps it is the wine, but I am serene, as if I am writing about someone else in whom I am intimately interested, yet distanced from. I am no longer paralyzed or fearful, as when I wrote the Governor. I have nothing to lose really, or perhaps I finally trust my mother's mantra that everything will be ok.

Dear Family Member of Nathan Wolfe:

My name is Stephanie Cassatly and I am writing to you with an unusual request. I am the daughter of Jeannette Marbán, the woman killed by Nathan in 1980. I was fortunate enough to have had the opportunity to forgive Nathan, and for him to apologize, before he passed away in Angola State Penitentiary in 2000. I went to Angola afterwards to visit his grave, but learned that his remains were sent to you.

I am currently in the final stages of writing a book about the life and death of my mother and the blessing of being able to forgive Nathan twenty years later. It was a healing and transformative experience for me, and him as well, I believe. I now know there were many victims the day my mother died, including you, your family and even Nathan. My book deals with the power and gift of forgiveness and my hope is that those who read it will consider it in their own lives.

One very important aspect of writing this book is my ability to humanize Nathan and understand who he was in his early life. When people hear and understand others' stories, they can often move from a place of hatred and anger to a place of compassion and even forgiveness. I wish I had asked Nathan more about his life before he went to prison and what brought him to the fateful day in 1980. I know only a little … that he was addicted to drugs and hallucinating, but I want to know more about his childhood, his family, etc … I believe this will deepen my story and help people to understand that we are all human, even if we make terrible choices and mistakes.

I understand that this may be a difficult and sensitive topic for you and that you may not wish to revisit this time period, however, it is my hope that I can share some of my peace with you and help others. I need your help to finalize this project and chapter in my life. Would you be willing to have a conversation (either in person or by phone), write or email me so that I can learn more? If you are willing, could you please contact me any way you feel most comfortable. My cell phone, address and email are enclosed.

I am contacting you from a place of grace and compassion and simply want to know a little more about Nathan's story prior to going to prison, so that I can portray him as a human being and not just a killer. Your assistance in this would be an enormous blessing to me, and hopefully others.

In Peace and Gratitude,

Stephanie

The next morning I walk out to the mailbox and mail the letters to the funeral home. Now there is nothing to do but wait. The next week feels vaguely reminiscent of the time after I made my initial call to Father La Beauve at the prison and he asked me to call him back in a week, only now I am not gripped with fear, just curious. I am a different person now.

As an aside, I also call Orleans Parish Court House to see if I can obtain the copy of Nathan's mug shot that the clerk offered several years ago. I believe I am ready to reconcile the image I fabricated of him with who he really was. I think I feel strong enough to see a headshot of him now, however not the other crime scene photos or the video. There are things I don't want to see or know, truths I want to keep buried. It's as if the body can only handle so much knowledge. The woman who takes my call tells me that all physical evidence, including photos, was destroyed in Katrina. "Everything was ten feet under water," she adds. I remember the images from television of a city under water and the worried phone calls to check on my aunts. I feel grateful somehow that I managed to get the transcript when I did. Perhaps, I'm even relieved that Nathan's physical self will always remain a ghost to me. I've become better at trusting that things work out as they should.

I go about my business as usual, work, exercise, friends, not really expecting that I will get a response from the letters I mailed, but a tiny window of hope remains open in my mind and heart. Even though Sarah and Hannah now know the story of my mother's death and how I forgave her killer, I mention this to no one but Michael. I don't want to fuel my old obsession with Nathan Wolfe.

The following Saturday, a letter arrives in my mailbox saying, 'Return to Sender.' It has the name Ruth Cooper and an address in Mission, Texas written on it. Inside is one of the letters I sent to the funeral home. I wonder if the other one was delivered. *Who is Ruth Cooper? His mother? His sister?* I wait a few more days thinking the other letter might get returned as well, but it doesn't. Perhaps it actually made it into the hands of Ruth Cooper. In the meantime, I surf the Internet and find the phone number for a Ruth Cooper, eighty-four years old, previously Ruth Wolfe, living in a nearby town in Texas. *This must be his mother*, I think. My mind is a jumble with what I might say and how I might begin such a conversation. Just as

I picked up the phone and spontaneously called Father La Beauve fifteen years ago, I do it again.

"Hello?"

"Is this Ruth Cooper?"

"Yes it is," she says in a thick southern accent.

"Ruth, my name is Stephanie. You don't know me, and I know this might come as a bit of a surprise, but I'm the daughter of the woman your son, Nathan, killed many years ago." There is no nice way to say this. As it rolls off my tongue, it sounds like an accusation, which I don't intend it to be. I want to say 'I come in peace,' but that sounds ridiculous. We are not at war. I hold nothing against her. But she does not know this.

There is a long pause at the other end of the phone and then she asks me to hold on a minute. I wonder if she is going to hang up or just not come back. I hear her tell a friend on another line that she will call her back.

"Listen," she says curtly and defensively when she returns. "I am very sorry for your loss, but I had nothing to do with what happened back then. He wasn't livin' at home and we didn't even know where he was until we got a phone call about what he done. It had nothin' to do with the way we raised him. That was a horrible time for us and I spent years just tryin' to move on."

I ask her if she can just give me a few minutes to explain myself.

"This is very upsettin' to me and I have to be somewhere in two minutes. That's all the time I got," she says.

I feel my heart rate quicken. At a loss for words I start stuttering and stammering, trying to convey that I don't blame her for anything, that I forgave Nathan before he died and that he expressed remorse, that I had sent her a letter asking for her to help me fill in some gaps with writing my story, that I am at peace and do not want to upset her. I feel as though I am trying to sell her something.

"Did you get my letter?" I ask her.

"Yes I did. To be honest, I thought it was a prank at first. It kinda threw me off balance for a minute, like I was gonna pass out. I kept goin' back to read it a few times."

All of a sudden I feel guilty for sending it, thinking how awful I'd feel if I caused this elderly woman to have a heart attack. A few years ago I might have considered it poetic justice; an eye for an eye ... he killed my mother, I kill his. But this is the farthest thing from my mind now.

"I'm so sorry, Ruth. I really don't mean to upset you."

"How old were you when she died?" her voice eases slightly.

"Eighteen," I say. There is another pause.

"You was young," she says softly, almost to herself. Perhaps she never thought about the family of the woman her son killed. Perhaps we all focus on our own losses.

"Yes."

She begins to offer up small bits of information. I quickly take hold of the phone with one hand and write notes on a nearby pad with the other. She tells me that she always felt she lost him twice: once when he went to prison and the second time when he died. They were a military family. They moved around a lot, like mine. How strange to think I could have anything at all in common with my mother's killer.

"Nathan always got in trouble. He always seemed to pick the wrong kinda friends everywhere we lived. We always found out after he messed up and he always said he was sorry, so it doesn't surprise me one bit that he said he was sorry to you." Ruth says she had two other children. An older daughter, Kathy, was already out of the house and married with children when Nathan went to prison, and a younger son, Robert, who was a police officer, of all things. Two sons: one good and one bad. Nathan was the middle child.

"Robert died of brain cancer when he was only forty-four years old," she continues. "We buried both our sons too young. Then my husband died ... I think it was all too much for him." *Two children and a husband ... that's a lot of loss for one woman,* I tally. "Then I got

218

married again. When I met my new husband, I had to tell him about Nathan goin' to prison and all. But he knew me by then and thankfully he was okay with it. But it wasn't easy." I suppose it wasn't. Every family has its shameful secrets. Even mine.

She explains that when Nathan first went to prison, she and his father visited him. Even though he had done such an unthinkable thing, it was crushing for them to know that he could never leave there. She recounts one visit when her husband cried and told him that if he could, he would trade places and serve his son's time. "That's how much he loved him." She also shares that she and her husband were there when Nathan died. I always thought he died alone.

"It's a horrible thing what Nathan did, but he paid a heavy price for it," she tells me. "If he hadn't of died, he'd still be there today."

"I know," I say, almost consoling her. How unexpected it is that I am comforting his mother for the sentence he justly deserved. I feel slightly hypocritical in this, but somehow I am able to see two sides of this coin, as if they are two different stories. I would not and could not ever have agreed to lighten his sentence, but I can also understand his mother's devastation. After all, I am a mother now and perhaps my visit to Angola has crystalized the severity of his punishment.

Ruth asks me about my family. I tell her I have a husband and two daughters and how they have saved me from my past. Something I've always said to Sarah and Hannah comes to mind and I offer it up to Ruth. "I always told my girls, 'I may not like what you do, but I'll always love you.'"

"That's a mother's love," she says. "No matter what Nathan did, he was always mine."

Oddly, that I constructed a different version of Nathan and his family so many years ago in order to help me humanize and forgive him, and that he was loved instead of abandoned, does not diminish how I feel. If anything, I feel something intensifying. This mother-to-mother connection and our common understanding of the unconditional nature of a mother's love, despite even the worst of a child's wrongdoing, feels like a radiant electrical wire running from her phone to mine, illuminating me from the inside out. I have gotten what I need.

The two minutes she afforded me have turned into forty-five. Many more questions swirl through my mind: *Is there a chance Nathan was mentally ill? Did you know he was a homosexual and a drug addict? Does mental illness or addiction run in your family? What other kind of trouble did he get into before committing murder?* But I withhold these questions out of respect for her age and her desire to move on, because they sound like accusations, which I am not interested in making and because it doesn't matter anyway.

Just before we hang up, she says to me, "I'm sorry you had to lose your mother when you was so young. That must have been really hard." And to that I respond, "I'm sorry you had to lose your son when he was so young. That must have been really hard too."

This morning I walk to my mailbox once again to mail a letter, but this time directly to Ruth Cooper, not some anonymous person via a funeral home. There are no more secrets or mysteries to be researched or revealed. I do not want to burden this elderly woman anymore, but there is one last thing I need to do. I write her a short note of thanks and include the medal of Saint Dismas, which I now know was always meant for her.

Afterward, I walk out to my dock, where a cooler breeze begins to blow across the Loxahatchee. It comes from a different direction now. Light and open, like a sail catching the wind, I sit drinking my first cup of coffee of the day.

Author's Note: In my research, I came across no pictures of Nathan Wolfe. I tried for many months to find one, with the intent of including it, as well as using his and other real names. However, between Hurricane Katrina and the pre Internet era of Nathan's life before prison (1960s and 1970s), there were none to be found.

Additionally, in my conversation with Ruth Cooper, I asked her if she would send me one, but she refused. She also asked me not to use his real name. Out of deference to her and for all the good that has come from writing my story, I do not wish to create any more pain. The intention of this book is to heal, not hurt. If nothing else, forgiving Nathan and writing this book have taught me to trust in something greater than myself, so perhaps Nathan was always meant to remain a ghost to me. Therefore, the names of Nathan Wolfe, Ruth Cooper, David Anderson, Russell Jones, Evan Shattick, Rachel and Marjorie have been changed at the request of family members and for the personal protection of my own family and me.

Coda
Forgiveness as the Color Grey

In the process of writing this book, I spent a great deal of time reading, thinking, speaking and learning about forgiveness, the central theme of my story. In the beginning, I only aspired to document my journey of forgiveness for my daughters and family and to help myself clarify its meaning in my life. Later, I realized my passion for writing and pursued my Masters in Fine Arts. If I possess any gift or ability for writing, I believe it evolved from the act of forgiving Nathan. As one door opens into another, forgiveness unlocked my mind and spirit. The following reflections are the culmination of what I believe on the topic and what I have learned along the way.

I believe forgiveness can only be defined in individual terms and that it can look quite different for each person. I also believe that strict dogma about forgiveness is not only a disservice to people who have been hurt, but to society as a whole. To say that we should always forgive or that some things are not forgivable is akin to black and white thinking. Such certainty on this complex topic is a type of absolute that is often one step away from extremism, intolerance and self-righteousness.

In the fall of 2014, I was serendipitously led to *The Forgiveness Project*, a UK based non-profit organization that examines themes of forgiveness, reconciliation and conflict transformation through powerful narratives collected from ordinary and diverse people around the world. I flew to London to meet the founder of the organization and author, Marina Catacuzino. She took me to lunch in a cozy diner just outside Paddington Station on a typical cold grey London winter day, where we spoke for several hours. After listening to my story and inviting me to be a contributor on the website, she said that "If forgiveness was a color, for [her] it would be the color grey, the color of compromise and conciliation, and because it sits between the two extremes of black and white." Coincidently, I was planning a talk about my experience of forgiving my mother's killer titled, "500 Shades of Forgiveness." I was interested to learn from Marina that the human eye can perceive not 50, but 500 shades of grey and the French impressionist painter, Odilon Redon, called grey the "soul of all color." She also shared the narrative and poignant words of an Israeli woman, Robi Damelin, another contributor, whose son was shot dead by a Palestinian sniper. Despite her crushing grief, Damelin so eloquently admitted of the Palestinian/Israeli conflict, "I wish I could view life through certain eyes of black and white and that the grey picture which keeps on creeping in would not shake up my opinions to remind me that I do not have a monopoly on truth." Forgiveness can be complicated, frightening, messy, rewarding or unrewarding and certainly not black and white.

All this being said, seven years after I forgave Nathan Wolfe and began my research to write this book, I was surprised, even shocked, to recognize that others who have traveled a path of forgiveness experienced similar and essential steps in their process. I had lived the process intuitively, quite unconsciously really, and only later formulated any notion of commonalities. The best depiction of this process that I have encountered is Desmond Tutu's "Fourfold Process," as seen in his book, *The Book of Forgiving*. Although quite similar to Desmond Tutu's model, which compares revenge to forgiveness, I have modified his model to incorporate six steps, as I personally experienced them and have heard from others.

The Process

For me, the path to forgiveness involved six steps:

1. Defining forgiveness
2. Exploring the story, including mine and Nathan's (as much as possible)
3. Recognizing a shared imperfect humanity
4. Discovering compassion
5. Offering forgiveness
6. Re-establishing or releasing the relationship

These steps can blend together and build upon each other, each leading to the next, almost in a domino effect. Once the first step is taken, the others can follow quite naturally. The path of not forgiving versus the path of forgiving might be compared to a closed system versus and open system and might visually look something like this.

STEPS TOWARDS FORGIVENESS

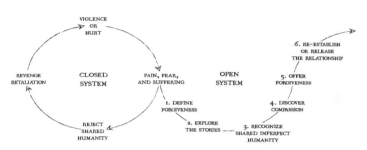

I noticed, however, that the steps are not necessarily sequential. Like grief, forgiveness may not be linear. Even after forgiving Nathan, I sometimes felt angry, hurt and sad all over again, wondering if I had really forgiven at all. Perhaps the best summation of this is Martin Luther King's statement, "Forgiveness is not a single act. It is a constant attitude." As evidenced fifteen years after forgiving Nathan and his subsequent death, when I spoke with his mother, Ruth Cooper, I revised my understanding of Nathan's story, felt more compassion and released the relationship all over again. Forgiveness is a fluid process, which happens in due time, in different ways, sometimes again and again and cannot be forced.

1. Defining Forgiveness

Like many complicated tasks, sometimes it's easier to back our way into them. For me, it was easier to make a list of what forgiveness was not:

- Forgiveness does not condone the act
- It does not erase or draw a veil over the hurt
- It does not accept that it was acceptable in any way
- It does not forget the act

- It does not favor lesser justice or legal consequences
- It does not often happen easily or quickly
- It does not require or even suggest any future relationship with the offender
- It does not excuse the act or behavior

So what is it then? What I found it to be, quite simply, was releasing all ill will or vengeance toward Nathan. It was the decision to not let him destroy my heart or hold me captive any longer. As Desmond Tutu says, "Forgiveness does not mean condoning what has been done. Forgiving means abandoning our right to pay back the perpetrator in his own coin."

Alternately, by holding onto hate, fear and vengeance, we continue to live (even glorify) the story and act, to empower pain, make ourselves sick, and even poison our relationships with others. This definition enabled me to take the next step in the process.

2. Exploring the Story

For years after my mother's death, I lived and operated from a place of pain and fear. It held me like a vice and penetrated virtually every aspect of my life. I knew what had happened to me, but I did not know what had happened in Nathan's life (nor did I care to). What I did not realize was that Nathan Wolfe also lived and operated from a place of pain. The same might also be said about my father, albeit one story does not equate to the other. They acted out in completely different ways, but both were prisoners of their pain.

Living from a place of pain is a closed system, a continuous cycle, where one hurt begets another, and suffering never ends. Hurt people hurt people, as layers of pain can cover the conscience. Whether we are perpetrators or victims, living in pain is an exhausting way to live. If we desire to live differently, it is important to not only acknowledge our own story, but to also try and learn (or imagine) the story of the person who hurt us. This can be difficult to unearth or hear, but it is an important step in breaking the cycle of pain and hurt, and moving toward peace.

I asked one of my excellent writing professors, Christopher Noel, "How do I write about something so painful?" He told me that in order to tell our difficult stories, we must "lean in and lean out" over and over again in order to bear the pain of difficult memories. We cannot stay in our dark places indefinitely, but by leaning in and out we stay balanced and gain perspective.

3. Recognizing a Shared Imperfect Humanity

Once I started to explore Nathan's story (and also my father's), I recognized their humanness and fallibility. Granted, not all harms are created equally. However, in my own honest introspection, I recognize that I have made mistakes and hurt others, and will continue to do so, as long as I am human. Therefore, on some level, we are all perpetrators and we are all victims. If we get so caught up in who is the biggest perpetrator or who is the bigger victim, we may drown in our own whirlpool of self-righteousness and judgment. Desmond Tutu advises, we should never say, 'I would never ...' Rather say, 'I hope that given the same set of circumstances, I would choose not to ..."

We must not lose sight of the fact that we are all interconnected and dependent on each other, like strands of a finely woven fabric. One tear in the fabric compromises the whole and we need each other to maintain the integrity of the fabric. The African term 'Ubuntu' speaks to this and is grounded in the idea that a person is a person through other people and strikes an affirmation of one's humanity through recognition of another. It suggests that humanity is not embedded in my person solely as an individual, but is a quality we owe to each other.

4. Discovering Compassion

Through learning something of Nathan's story and acknowledging his humanity, including his imperfections, a small door was opened for compassion. He had grown up in a military family, with a strict father who probably did not accept his son's homosexuality. A parent's rejection is a powerful hurt for a child. Nathan became a drug addict, perhaps to block out his own pain. He lost his connection to his own humanity, acting out in ways that destroyed not only his life, but also the lives of others.

Another contributor to The Forgiveness Project, Samantha Lawler, who forgave her father before he died in prison many years after killing her mother, shares that "compassion is the gateway to forgiveness." The word compassion derives from the Latin word "Compati," which means to suffer with, listen deeply and understand. Her father was in a deep state of suffering when she reconnected with him, and through this suffering, she was able to feel compassion for him, despite his terrible and hurtful act years earlier.

5. Offering Forgiveness

When we open the door to the possibility of compassion, we open the door to the possibility of forgiveness. It's amazing how one leads quite naturally to the next.

As Samantha Lawler added about her own story of forgiving her father, "I didn't forgive the act, I forgave the person." Her father was an imperfect person. So was Nathan Wolfe. So was my father. So am I. So are we all.

After hearing my story, people often comment that forgiving Nathan (and even my father) was such a courageous act, so generous and selfless. They don't think they could do it. I am perplexed by this, because from my standpoint, it was an act of self-preservation and ultimately self-serving. For me, forgiveness offered the possibility and hope of a better life than the one I was living. In the words of writer Paul Boese, "Forgiveness does not change the past, but it does enlarge the future."

6. Re-establishing or Releasing the Relationship

Because Nathan Wolfe died soon after I forgave him, I released the relationship. Even if he had lived, there would have been nothing to re-establish, as we were strangers. I sometimes wonder, however, if he had lived, whether we would have had any further communication. As I've learned from others, sometimes the most unbelievable relationships evolve from the act of forgiveness. Victims travel with offenders to speaking engagements, or work side by side to prevent future crimes or promote certain messages. It is incredible to learn about and it speaks volumes of the transformative power of forgiveness.

For many people, depending on the circumstances, this last step can be a choice. Whether establishing for the first time, re-establishing or releasing the relationship, all are valid and can return power and peace to the victim.

Remorse

The topic of remorse is of great interest to me. Many years ago when Father La Beauve asked me, "Does it make any difference if Nathan feels remorse?" I pondered this question for a long time. "What does remorse have to do with forgiveness and how important is it?"

Desmond Tutu speaks of two models of forgiveness: one with remorse and one without. Remorse as a condition for forgiveness is the most familiar model. It is when we say "I am willing to forgive you if you say sorry." It is often seen in models of restorative justice. It essentially requires remorse as the payback for our gift of forgiveness and is considered a negotiation of sorts. While this model can be more gratifying, resolute and effective, it is not always possible. For example, if someone we love is hurt or killed by a hit and run driver, we may never know if the driver has remorse for what he or she did. Another limitation of this model is that there are strings attached to the act of forgiving and these strings still tether or bind us to our perpetrators.

The second model of forgiveness is one without remorse, where forgiveness is given unconditionally as an act of grace or an unmerited gift. In history, this is probably best exemplified by Christ on the cross saying, "Forgive them Father for they know not what they do." But there are many other examples, both famous and not so famous, of this model. In this model of forgiveness, there are no strings attached. While this may be more difficult or take more work, the victim is released from being bound in any way to the perpetrator.

In my case, it turned out Nathan was remorseful, but I initiated the call to forgive him *before* I knew whether he was or not. I needed to get out of pain regardless of his remorse. I believe either model can release us from our own personal prisons. Regardless of which model one uses, Max Lucado says, "Forgiveness is unlocking the door to set someone free and realizing you were the prisoner."

Faith

The question of whether one has to have faith to forgive is another interesting topic to explore. Having been born and raised a Catholic, I see that Christianity certainly provides plenty of examples needed to support the act of forgiving. However, as evidenced by the many stories in *The Forgiveness Project,* and by the founder herself, I believe that the process of forgiveness is universal and non-sectarian.

Abrahamic faiths (Islam, Judaism, Christianity) all offer teachings on forgiveness. The Torah, the Bible, and the Qur'an all have dictates on what God forgives, and what human beings should bestow upon each other.

Non-Abrahamic faiths also have approaches to forgiveness that are not so different from modern, secular or psychological treatments of the subject. Buddhism, for example, teaches that people who hold on to the wrongs done to them create an identity around that pain, and that identity continues to manifest and be reborn.

While I personally believe that a higher power works within our lives, I also believe that forgiveness is based not so much on faith alone, but on faith in humanity. Anyone can offer it and anyone can receive it.

Timing

People ask 'How long does forgiveness take?' In my experience, it took a very long time. Twenty years to be exact. It took as long as it took, and there were no short cuts.

While there may be no predictable timetable, perhaps it can be said that smaller wounds can be forgiven more quickly, but deeper wounds can take much longer. As mentioned earlier, the effect of forgiving when not ready or too quickly can translate to insincerity and do more harm than good. If the timing is not correct, a victim can feel even more violated, as if giving away his or her power. It is important to be patient with the process and ourselves.

<u>Final Thoughts</u>

I believe forgiveness is a deeply personal issue that no one can tell another to do or not to do. There are so many hurts in this world, some seemingly insurmountable, and we must each navigate our own as best we can. I also believe, however, that whether we are the ones who have been hurt or done the hurting, it matters how we behave in both situations. We all have a choice in this regard. Forgiveness can be a living practice we choose to cultivate, no matter how big or small the hurt. No one can tell us what to do or how to do it, but we can certainly open our minds up to the possibility of living better, more peaceful lives. It is within everyone's reach.

Acknowledgments

Although I am named as author, this book would not exist if not for the generous and loving support of so many others, all of whom I cannot name. Many minds and hearts brought this writing to fruition and I am forever grateful.

The seeds of this book were germinated on the fertile grounds of Vermont College of Fine Arts and expertly nurtured by my teacher, mentor, author and friend, Sue Silverman, who saw the potential for this book before I did and pulled it out of me. I also owe a debt of gratitude to other teachers and guides, Phyllis Barber, Christopher Noel and Director, Louise Crowley. You all taught me everything I know about writing.

I struggled for a long time to find the right home for my memoir, and realize now that eLectio Publishing was the right place for it all along. Thank you Jesse Greever, Christopher Dixon and everyone at eLectio for seeing the good that this book might bring into the world. I am also deeply grateful to the production team and fellow writers who make up the eLectio Family.

Thank you to my many readers, in particular, Lynn Hays, an insightful editor and sister of my heart, who tirelessly and enthusiastically read many versions of this story and traveled alongside me every step of my journey. Thank you also Diane Martinez, Susan Jones, Anne Granieri, Evonn Loren, Hilda Porro, Susan Goldstein, Simone and Pete McPhee, Leayne Eble, Matt and Eileen Rostock, Marian Galbraith, Claire and Yousef Valine, Etienne and Laura DuBarry, Rob Weagle, Karen Braccini, Joyce Serventi, Joe and Joyce Cassatly, Linda Fore, Nancy and Jim Harvey, Genevieve Caron, Anna Nemes, Beate Rodewald, Patrice Austin and my wonderfully astute book club for close readings on various incarnations of this story, brainstorming ideas and moral support when I was adrift within this project.

Thanks also to Tonya Beach, my friend and talented graphic artist who conceived the cover for this book, Paul Fattori and Tammy Toro Rosenthal for their technological, photographic and creative genius, and David Athey and Robin Oliveira for their early guidance in publishing. In this same vein, I would like to thank Sarah Cantin and Margaret King Riley as well.

To the Reverend Jim Cook of St. Mark's Episcopal Church and Marina Catacuzino of The Forgiveness Project, thank you for giving me the space to first tell my story publicly. In addition to my entire St. Mark's family, I owe a debt of gratitude to Gary Crenshaw, the Reverend Kerry Robb and the Reverend Jeannie Martz for first introducing me to the concept of real forgiveness. To Arno Michaelis and Samantha Lawler, thank you for sharing your own journeys to forgive, for expanding my understanding of the topic and for reaffirming the power of compassion and inclusion.

To Gary Young, Kathy Fontenot and Father Joel La Beauve at Louisiana State Penitentiary (Angola) and George Charlet of Charlet Funeral Home, thank you for your patience and willingness to help me explore, as best you could, the life and death of my mother's killer, and for helping me gain access to a restricted world so little known or understood. It enriched my understanding, healing and story immensely.

Thank you to my family, Joy Drago, Annie Purcell, Susie Payne, Stephen, Holly, Carlos and Lisa Marban, Heather Flynn, Rita Powell and Suzanne Chirico, for encouraging me to explore our past, even if it made you uncomfortable at times. I have done my best to be truthful, yet realize my memories may be different than yours. I have tried to tread lightly upon some of our minefields, but where I did not, please forgive me. Your love and support mean the world to me.

To Kathy and Jack Borbely, thank you for your unending inclusiveness and grace. To Katelyn Borbely, whose creativity and generosity never cease to amaze me, thank you for always saying yes. To the Flynn family, thank you for your friendship and support.

Last, but certainly not least, I want to thank my best friend and husband, Michael, and my daughters, Hannah and Sarah, for your eternal support, many readings and life-giving love. You are my greatest cheerleaders, my guiding lights, the loves of my life, and my reason for being.

Reading Sources

A Grief Like No Other – Surviving the Violent Death of Someone You Love, by Kathleen O'Hara

The Book of Forgiving, by Desmond Tutu and Mpho Tutu

Cain's Redemption – A Story of Hope and Transformation in America's Bloodiest Prison, by Dennis Shere

The Forgiveness Project – Stories for a Vengeful Age, by Marina Catacuzino

The Sunflower - On the Possibilities and Limits of Forgiveness, by Simon Wiesenthal

Motherless Daughters – The Legacy of Loss, by Hope Edelman

My Dark Places, James Ellroy

Within These Walls – Memoirs of a Death House Chaplain, Rev. Carrol Pickett

Made in the USA
Middletown, DE
23 April 2017